West Highland Way

The author and publisher have made every effort to ensure that the information in this publication is accurate, and accept no responsibility whatsoever for any loss, injury, inconvenience, midge bites or blisters experienced by any person or persons whilst using this book.

We aim to update our guides every year, so if something has changed that you think we should know about or if we've got something wrong, please email us at info@pocketmountains.com. If your update is included in the next edition we will send you a free copy.

published by
pocket mountains ltd
6 Church Wynd, Bo'ness EH51 0AN
pocketmountains.com

ISBN-978-0-9554548-5-1

Text copyright © Dan Bailey 2008

Photography copyright © Dan Bailey 2008, except pages 6, 11, 12, 16, 18, 20, 22, 24, 26, 34, 36, 40, 46, 66, 68, 76 © Robbie Porteous 2008

With thanks to Mike McManus of the Loch Lomond & The Trossachs National Park Authority.

The right of Dan Bailey to be identified as the Author of this work has been asserted by him in accordance with the Copyright, Designs and Patents Act 1988

A catalogue record for this book is available from the British Library

All route maps are based on 1945 Popular Edition Ordnance Survey material and revised from field surveys by Pocket Mountains Ltd, 2007-8. © Pocket Mountains Ltd 2007-8.

Printed in Poland

Introduction

'Have you done the West Highland Way?' If you're talking about walking with someone who doesn't, that's probably one of the first things they'll ask. No other long-distance path has such celebrity status, and it is the country's most famous hike for good reason. Officially opened in 1980, the West Highland Way is Scotland's original long-distance footpath, and still the best. Over the last quarter of a century it has become a symbol of the Scottish outdoors, practically an institution in its own right. A reputation as one of the great walks of the world attracts visitors from all corners. Rightly so. Over its 152km (95-mile) length, the route winds through a rich variety of landscapes – pastoral lowlands, woods and loch shores, moor and mountain. The path links the country's largest and most vibrant city with its highest peak. Along the way it visits Scotland's first National Park, runs beside its best-loved loch, takes in a corner of its wildest moor and crosses the mouth of its most atmospheric glen. Large sections of the West Highland Way follow the course of older routes, disused railway lines, military roads, cattle drovers' tracks: in this way it connects us with those who came before. History, wildlife and spectacular scenery – each day brings something new.

Although the surroundings are often rugged, the path itself doesn't demand particular fitness or skill. Signposts and waymarks keep you firmly on track; transport links make access relatively straightforward; shops, pubs and places to stay are not so widely spaced that life gets inconvenient. Thanks in part to these amenities, the popularity of the West Highland Way is growing steadily: estimates suggest that it now receives upwards of 50,000 visitors annually. If that sounds like your idea of hell, then bear in mind that most people are only out for a quick stroll, and the minority who actually walk the full route are spread over 152km and 365 days. Outwith the short high season, it's possible to have a much quieter experience.

While accomplished walkers will take the challenge in their stride, a long multi-day through-route such as this represents a major goal to work towards for anyone more used to an afternoon stroll – but one that is ultimately more satisfying. You should experience a strong sense of continuity as the country unrolls beneath your feet day after day – a spectacular way either to get better acquainted with your own country or gain a first introduction to the Highlands. Far from closing a chapter, though, completing the West Highland Way should open your eyes to more possibilities: with a series of inspiring detours along the route, this guide should entice you back to the finest stretches of the Way again and again.

About this guide

For a path with two ends, it might seem odd to talk about a start and a finish. After all, there's no law against beginning in Fort William and winding up in Milngavie, and a few mavericks do just that. But they're the walking equivalent of salmon, swimming against the flow. The convention is to start in the south and

finish in the north, and with the prevailing weather at your back and the mountains ahead to beckon you on, northwards is the natural direction to go. It's how we've ordered this book.

We have divided the route into eight main sections because it is the clearest and most logical way to describe it. You really don't have to do the same. Keen long-distance walkers could comfortably knock off the West Highland Way in as few as four days: it is often run in well under 24 hours, after all. But there's nothing to stop you from taking as long as you like – and by including a number of off-trail detours along the way, the route could be strung out over 10 very satisfying days.

The description of each stage of the trail begins with a brief fact panel that covers the type of terrain you'll encounter that day, recommends an appropriate map for anyone wishing to stray from the path and quantifies the total distance to be walked and the number of metres climbed. The distance and ascent figures take into account key off-route legs into Crianlarich and Drymen. Both are a short distance from the West Highland Way proper, though you're likely to visit for them for supplies or accommodation. What we don't offer is an estimate of how long each stage of the path will take you, since this is very much down to the ability and whim of the individual walker. Likewise, because the path is so well

Gaelic glossary

abhainn	river
allt	stream
aonach	mountain ridge
beag	small
bealach	mountain pass
beinn	mountain
bidean	pinnacle
buachaille	herdsman
caisteal	castle
càrn	cairn
clachan	hamlet
cnoc	hillock
coire	corrie
creachann	rocky summit
creag	cliff
dearg	red
dubh	black
dun	hill fortress
eag	notch
eilean	island
garbh	rough
lairig	pass
lochan	small loch/pool
mòr	big
sgòrr	peak

signed from start to finish, a minutely detailed set of step-by-step instructions is unnecessary. The route description you'll find here should give you plenty to go on without asking you to spend half of each day with your nose buried in a guidebook when you could be enjoying the scenery. Places of particular interest are highlighted in box-out sections peppered through the text, along with introductory

snippets for first-time visitors on the history and geography of the landscapes you'll encounter. It seems a shame to pass through the mountains without climbing any of them, so some detours to notable summits are described: most of these are serious hillwalking trips, generally taking at least half a day. Low-level detours are also included.

When to go
Weather, daylight hours, midges and crowds are all factors that might influence when you choose to go.

Weather Thanks to its changeable maritime climate, the weather in the Highlands is always unpredictable, and if you're planning a trip in advance no period can be 100 percent relied upon to be fine and dry. Come expecting the worst, and you might be rewarded with the best. Prevailing westerly weather systems tend to bring plenty of wet and wind at any time of year, but clear calm periods occur more frequently than the popular caricature of the Scottish weather might lead you to

Mountain biking
While it may not meet with every walker's approval, there is nothing to stop mountain bikers also taking up the challenge of the West Highland Way. Some sections of the route are easy to ride and attract two-wheeled traffic, but others are much harder and require shouldering the bike for long stretches; the Loch Lomond section is particularly tiresome in this regard. Anyone attempting to bike the route in one day will find it extremely tough and should carry plenty of spares. The vast majority of riders are responsible and will let you know they are passing. If you hear their bell, however, remember to hold your course – the bell means they can see you, so don't step to the side and potentially into their path.

believe, and these also happen in every season. As a rough generalisation it's fair to expect much of winter to be cold and wet, and midsummer to be warm and wet. Long fine periods tend to crop up between mid-spring and June, and again in early autumn. But please don't quote us on that.

◂ Mountain biker near Dumgoyne

Daylight hours November and December are the dourest, darkest months. At these northerly latitudes, midwinter daylight hours dwindle to as little as seven per day. That doesn't leave long to squeeze in a full day's walk, but the upside is that there's a lot of night-time to while away in the pub. At the opposite extreme, mid-June brings more than 17 hours of daylight in every 24.

Midges Thriving in the damp vegetation that cloaks much of the country north of Glasgow, these tiny bloodsucking parasites swarm in countless millions, bringing misery and madness to anyone hapless enough to get in their way. Mid-June to late August is their bumper season, though midges (or midgies) respect no timetable and can often be found outside this period too. You've not been properly midged until every bit of exposed flesh is hopping with them, your scalp feels like it's crawling and you're inhaling clouds of insects with every breath. Some people find that midge bites remain itchy for several days, while for others the effects are barely noticeable. They tend to prefer sheltered hollows and still, humid weather around dawn and dusk. At these times you'll be grateful for a headnet: you might even wish you'd gone for the full beekeeper's suit. Conventional insect repellents are of little use, but some report limited success with Avon's Skin So Soft moisturiser: if nothing else, you'll have baby soft hands

with which to swat your tormentors. However, the best prevention remains avoidance. Keep moving, sleep indoors or camp in windy spots. And don't let the midge's reputation put you off. Life is too short to base your holidays around the breeding cycle of a few insects, after all.

Crowds Combining generally reasonable weather with the added advantage of fairly few midges, May is understandably high season for West Highland Way-ers. At this time, accommodation books up weeks in advance and the trail is unlikely to be quiet and uncrowded – unless you're into midnight rambling, of course. Starting midweek from Milngavie might mean a less cluttered path and more chance of finding vacant beds, as walkers tend to begin en masse at weekends and move along the route at roughly similar speeds, creating a once-weekly surge at every B&B and hostel. Despite the tendency for damp weather and the best efforts of the midges, the midsummer tourist season is also extremely busy, with a great many cars on the roads as well as hikers on the hills. Bearing all the other seasonal factors in mind, if you want to avoid crowds then consider April or September.

Weatherproof walkers might enjoy early spring, late autumn or even full-on winter. During this half of the year, you're likely to have the West Highland Way more or less to yourself. The weather might be wild, of course, but if you're lucky enough to catch a fine spell then you will enjoy a memorable (and, what's more, midge-free) experience.

Another timing issue that may not immediately spring to mind concerns motorbikes, believe it or not. The Scottish Six Days Trial is an annual extreme motorsports event held in Lochaber in early May. It makes use of sections of the West Highland Way. For details of when not to be there, see ssdt.org.

Accommodation

Night-time possibilities include campsites, youth hostels and independent bunkhouses, B&Bs and even the odd hotel. These are scattered all along the West Highland Way, though sometimes fairly spaced. This book refers to the more obvious choices, with particular attention given to budget accommodation. Wild camping is a good option for the hardy, though this should be kept as low impact as possible. Toilet waste is a real problem in busy areas such as Loch Lomond, and rubbish should always be carried out with

you. The bothy is a longstanding Scottish tradition. These are informal mountain huts located in out-of-the-way spots, providing basic free accommodation for anyone who comes along. There are only two on the direct course of the footpath.

Mountain skills

One great attraction of the West Highland Way is that it takes you through scenes of mountain grandeur without requiring any specialist skills, such as compass navigation. Stick to the official path through the glens and you need nothing more than this guidebook and the frequent waymarks to stay on track.

The hill detours described in this book can't be treated so lightly. These take you into wild, rough country – remote, desolate and lightly populated. Highland weather can change rapidly and often for the worse: heavy rain is frequent throughout the year and snow on the summits is not unknown, even in mid-summer. Visibility can quickly deteriorate from crystal clear to just a few metres. Above the glen floor, the terrain is steep and treacherous, and paths sometimes indistinct. Unlike many parts of the world, there are generally no signposts in Scottish hills: when not on the West Highland Way you have to take responsibility for orienting yourself. Detailed maps (usually at 1:50,000 or 1:25,000 scale) should be considered a necessity, as should a compass – and the ability to use it properly.

Falls are one obvious source of danger, but perhaps of greater concern is hypothermia. It is common for first-time visitors to the Highlands to under-estimate the area's typical windy, cold and damp weather, yet it chills the body far quicker than the drier and often (on paper) more extreme cold of continental

Public transport

- Glasgow and Fort William are connected by an A-road and a railway: the West Highland Way is effectively a third transport link in its own right, for those who aren't in a hurry. All three meet up at Crianlarich, Tyndrum and Bridge of Orchy. Ardlui Station is also not far off the route at the top of Loch Lomond. There are usually three trains a day from Fort William to Glasgow and the spectacular journey takes around four hours (firstgroup.com/scotrail).
- Milngavie is not on this line but is well served by trains from Glasgow Queen Street leaving every 30 minutes (firstgroup.com/scotrail).
- A Glasgow to Fort William bus service is operated by Citylink and takes around three hours. The bus will also stop at Inverarnan, Crianlarich, Tyndrum and the White Corries in Glencoe on the way (citylink.co.uk).
- FirstGroup run regular buses from Milngavie to Drymen (8) (firstgroup.com) and you can get from Drymen to Balmaha on a McColl's bus (309) (mccolls.org.uk).
- During the summer season several small ferry operators can take you across Loch Lomond from Rowardennan, Inversnaid and Ardleish to Inverbeg, Tarbet or Inveruglas, and Ardlui respectively. Contact the local hotels to organise in advance.
- A Royal Mail Postbus leaves Inversnaid around midday every weekday bound for Aberfoyle.
- Highland bus company Rapsons run a daily service from Kinlochleven to Fort William (44, 44B) and from the Lower Falls in Glen Nevis to Fort William from May to September (rapsons.co.uk).

mountain ranges. Combine this with tiredness and low blood sugar and you could end up in trouble, even in August. The solution is to keep moving, stay well fed, go properly equipped and avoid getting lost. Simple, really.

Clothing and equipment

First-time backpackers often carry far more than they need, 'just in case', and end up with a bulging sack dangling pots and pans that clang like cowbells as they stagger along with red faces. If you want your enjoyment of the trip to be more than masochistic, then kitchen sink syndrome should be avoided. Strip it down and keep it light. That said, you've probably taken the lightweight philosophy too far when you start cutting off the handles of spoons and tooth-brushes to shave a few grams. This is a footpath, not the north face of the Eiger, after all. You could spend a small fortune in outdoor shops in preparation for the West Highland Way, yet there are really only a few basic essentials:

Footwear For large parts of its length the West Highland Way follows level, well-drained tracks that you could casually stroll along in a pair of trainers – and many do just that. Sturdy 'approach shoes' or trail-running shoes are adequate for most, if not all, of the route. Although they are by far the best bet on hard surfaces such as gravel and tarmac, shoes do have obvious drawbacks in wet weather

> ## Baggage carriers
> If the thought of seven days or more carrying a fully-laden rucksack does not appeal then you will be glad to know that the West Highland Way is well served by dedicated baggage carriers. For a modest fee (around £30-35) a van will pick up your rucksack from your B&B, hostel or campsite in the morning, and deliver it to your next port of call, where it'll be waiting for you at the end of the day. Some may call this cheating, others common sense. Two very reliable local firms offer this service: **AMS Scotland** (amsscotland.co.uk) and **Travel-lite** (travel-lite-uk.com).

or on ankle-twisting rough ground. Occasionally the path is boggy or uneven enough that sturdier walking boots are a good idea. When selecting a pair of boots remember that lightweight and comfy beats heavy and clumpy hands (or feet) down. The one possible exception to this is on mountain detours, particularly in winter. Whatever footwear you settle on make sure that it fits well, as you'll be stuck with it for 152km. If your boots are new then give these and your feet time to get used to each other before leaving home. This might seem obvious, yet it is surprising how many people suffer in brand new over-stiff boots bought especially for their trip: blisters are sheer misery, and can make life on trail into the trial of your life. One possible ruse is to bring both boots and shoes, swapping

View from the King's House in Glencoe ▶

them around as the weather, the terrain and your developing blisters dictate. OK, it's not minimalist packing, but come day four you might be glad you were so prudent.

Clothing As emphasised in the skills section, you shouldn't come to the Highlands at any time of year without expecting cold, wet and windy weather. Modern 'soft shells' may look trendy in the Alps, but they are of limited use in a Scottish downpour. The good old-fashioned principle of layering is a handy one to follow, since you can add or remove items to suit the conditions. Start with an underlayer – synthetic or wool T-shirt or thermal top designed to 'wick' sweat away from the body to keep you dry; a warm layer comes next, most often a synthetic fleece; top off the ensemble with a shell of breathable waterproof jacket and trousers. A couple of warm spares are a good idea, stashed safe and dry in the rucksack for that all-too-likely full-body soaking. In spring, autumn or winter (and also summer, some would say) a hat and gloves should be carried. A pair of trousers with zip-off legs that lets them double as

shorts is worth considering in summer. For all of these items, avoid cotton, which soaks up moisture and makes you cold. Jeans especially are inadvisable – Levi them at home.

Bits and bobs The amount of other stuff you carry is optional, though in general the less the better. Walking poles help spare the knees; a penknife can prove handy; no one should go anywhere without a long piece of string, though its exact use may never be fully clear. A torch (ideally a headtorch) is worth having, even if it only comes out of the bag for the late-night stumble back from a pub. A compass is a must for walkers intending to climb some hills along the way. So too is a survival bag or bivi bag for every member of the party: given an immobilising injury or an unplanned

11

night out, this provides life-saving protection from the elements. Hill detours in winter conditions often require ice axe, crampons and a basic level of mountaineering competence. If in doubt, don't go out.

Campers obviously need rather more than those aiming to spend their nights indoors. Though most of this will be obvious stuff like tents and sleeping bags, it's also worth bearing in mind that food shops are sometimes few and far between, and that self-caterers may end up carrying supplies for several days in addition to all their gear.

Wildlife

Stony summits, heather moorland, peat bogs, woodland and lochs – the varied habitats of the Highlands provide a haven for a wide range of flora and fauna. Wildlife lovers will be in their element. With luck (and patience), it's possible to spot all sorts of beasties, including golden eagles, capercaillie, ravens, buzzards, grouse, ptarmigan, red deer, roe deer, feral goats, foxes, badgers, pine marten, red squirrels, mountain hares, otters and even – so it is said – wildcats. Unconfirmed sightings of wild haggis scuttling around in the mist have usually been linked with excessive whisky consumption. Even among the genuine species, some animals are rarer and more elusive than others, so if the best you can boast is a couple of buzzards and the odd red deer then don't be disappointed.

Environment

The vast sparsely populated expanse of the Highlands encompasses some of the most scenic and least spoilt landscapes remaining in Europe, a priceless wild land resource both for UK residents and for visitors from around the world. Considering its international significance, the preservation of this environment ought to go without saying; yet sadly this is not everywhere the case. In recent years hard-won National Park status for the Cairngorms and Loch Lomond and the Trossachs has conferred

◄ Feral goats near Inversnaid

a new (if not total) level of defence from large development projects such as windfarms and electricity pylons. However, most of the Highlands remains outside these ring-fenced areas, enjoying only piecemeal protection – if any at all. This seems inconsistent, as any walker on the West Highland Way may note as they pass out of the Loch Lomond & the Trossachs National Park into surroundings far less protected and yet no less magnificent. Ben Lomond is rightly incorporated within a National Park, so why not the incomparable tundra-like expanse of Rannoch Moor or the superbly rugged mountains of Glencoe? In recent years, the number of renewable energy projects and powerlines proposed for the Highlands has mushroomed. Whatever your take on green power, it can't be denied that these developments are currently unprecedented in scale and scope, and will effectively industrialise swathes of hitherto wild land. Every technology has an environmental footprint – the key in this case is arguably to zone it sensitively, with an eye to preserving the unique qualities of the Scottish mountain landscape at all costs.

Getting involved in such big debates is all very well (and perhaps more people ought to do it!), but at a fundamental level protection for the mountain environment depends upon our behaviour as individuals. With so many people gravitating to one trail the effects of bad practice are concentrated, and it's arguably all the more important to be conscientious on the West Highland Way. So here comes the lecture. Not dropping any litter, and picking up other people's, is a no-brainer. This includes things like orange peel and banana skins, neither of which decompose quickly. Lighting campfires is questionable, especially on such a busy route. Use a proper toilet wherever you can, but if you must go outdoors then don't do it near any watercourses – it's not a nice thing for other people to drink. If the matter at hand is rather more substantial than a quick pee behind a bush, then bury the evidence. A pile of stones squished on top isn't good enough: animals may unearth whatever you've left, and it doesn't break down that readily on the surface. Burn all toilet paper, obviously being careful not to leave it smouldering.

Even something as apparently innocuous as putting one foot in front of the other can be interpreted as an environmental issue. With thousands of tramping boots, path erosion is a real problem on some stretches. To minimise your footprint, stick to the middle of the main trail, and shun any shortcuts or parallel paths. If at the end of the walk, you travel home by public transport (trains beat planes and automobiles) then feel free to indulge in a spot of self-congratulatory back patting.

The route

Route maps

At a scale of 1:50,000, Ordnance Survey Landranger maps may be indispensable on the hill-climbing detours in this book (*see page 49*), but to cover the entire course of the West Highland Way you'd need five separate sheets; numbers 41, 50, 56, 57 and 64. That's quite a bit of paper to lug around; and just think of the poor trees. For those intending to walk only the official path without any significant detours and wanting the reassurance of a detailed map, the best bet is the Harvey dedicated West Highland Way XT40 map, which cleverly covers the entire route (although only a limited corridor of flanking country) on a single lightweight waterproof sheet.

Access

Scotland enjoys some of the most liberal access legislation in the world. The public right to use open hill country, privately owned or not, is enshrined in law under the Land Reform (Scotland) Act of 2003. It's worth noting, however, that legal access still comes with strings attached. The law refers pointedly to 'responsible access', which is fundamentally just a formal term for common sense and consideration.

To abide by the spirit of the legislation use paths where available, do not enter gardens, don't camp within sight of houses, never climb fences, don't disturb livestock or agriculture and steer well clear of any forestry or deer stalking activities. Other than that, Scotland's countryside is all yours, and free to enjoy. Find out more by visiting outdooraccess-scotland.com

Milngavie to Drymen

Distance 19.5km **Ascent** 160m **Terrain** mainly flat and low-lying; good paths, some tarmac

Most people catch a train from Glasgow to Milngavie (pronounced *Mull-guy*) at the beginning of the West Highland Way. But if 152km doesn't sound like enough of a challenge, then you could always kick-start your holiday with a brisk hike from the city centre. Starting at Central Station it's possible to link the Clyde, Kelvin and Allander Walkways, waymarked riverside routes that take in some interesting urban sights and several parks in a 19km meander that leads – eventually – to the main event.

Milngavie itself is a leafy suburb of Glasgow, and though pleasant enough it doesn't on first sight seem to be the obvious starting point for Scotland's

greatest long-distance walk. The Highlands are as yet nowhere to be seen. A small stone obelisk on Douglas Street marks the official start of the route, conveniently close to a bank, a couple of bakeries and the Iron Chef, a hardware shop selling camping gas, midge repellent and other last-minute supplies; don't get too used to this abundance of amenities.

Outside town, things soon start to feel a little more auspicious as you follow the rushing Allander Water into Mugdock Country Park. The old oak woodlands here are typical of Scotland's west coast, and incorporate a site of special scientific interest (SSSI), rich in flora and fauna. In high summer they are lush with ferns and mosses. Beyond the woods, you soon leave Milngavie's dog walkers and joggers behind. The path runs alongside a wide

◄ Milngavie's very
own Sinatra and the
start of the WHW

The Carbeth Hutters

Though common in Scandinavia,
small private country huts are a rare
sight in Scotland these days. The
habit of 'hutting' emerged during the
economic depression of the interwar
period, when people in Glasgow and other
cities started claiming access to the
countryside. The huts at Carbeth and similar
communities elsewhere were self built,
completely informal, and offered a temporary
escape from urban poverty. At weekends and
holidays each might be occupied by dozens
of members of the same family. Many people
decamped there for the duration of the
second war, when Glasgow suffered heavy
bombing. Hutters own their chalets, but rent
the land that they stand on. Most hut
communities have now been cleared; recently
things also looked bleak for Carbeth, and yet
it has hung on and remains the country's
largest surviving hutter community.

marshy area by the Allander Water. It then
passes quiet Craigallian Loch and a
'village' of wooden chalets by the side of
Carbeth Loch.

Soon after is a short open stretch that
can be exposed to bad weather, passing a
craggy wooded knoll (Dumgoyach) to
reach the wide floodplain of Strath Blane.

The path now follows the course of an old
railway line that went out of service over
50 years ago; it plots a straight and very
level course for several kilometres. The
walking itself is undistinguished, and you
could be forgiven for thinking that a bike

would be nice. But at least the views are good, including Glengoyne Distillery steaming gently beneath the little peak of Dumgoyne, a distinctive squat, craggy landmark. Depending whether you prefer hard exercise or hard spirits, either might be worth a visit (*see detour p50*); the distillery is only a few minutes off-route, for those who fancy a tour and a tasting.

It is still a long way to Drymen, through miles of fertile farmland. This is arguably the least exciting section of the entire walk, best seen as a prelude to the good stuff to come, and a chance to get into the swing of things. A nip of whisky might help the miles roll by. If it's raining, the weir and waterfall at Gartness can be

impressive. Just beyond, you enter Loch Lomond & the Trossachs National Park, 1865 square kilometres of protected land encompassing some of the finest scenery in Scotland. The Highlands now seem close, and with luck the most southerly peaks will be visible ahead. Quiet lanes running between hedgerows recall the Devon countryside, and lead almost all the way from Gartness to the outskirts of Drymen.

Though the path officially bypasses Drymen this pretty, friendly little place is only a few minutes away, and provides a good excuse to call it a day. The village has a history dating back to at least 1238. As well as B&Bs, two hotels and Rob Roy's

Tartan gangsters

In the 18th century, the notorious cattle rustling clan MacGregor (of Rob Roy fame) operated a protection racket in Drymen. They'd regularly descend from the mountains to the village green, where local farmers were more or less obliged to provide them with cattle. In exchange for this concession the MacGregors undertook to recover stock stolen by other raiders, and promised not to steal any more themselves – good in theory, perhaps, though the lowland farmers had no choice in the matter. If it seems strange that such gangsterism has since been romanticised, remember that those were days of savage inter-clan rivalries and standards were rather different. The MacGregors had fallen on hard times, dispossessed and harried by rival 'gangs'. Stealing cattle was a way of life when few other choices were available.

local, the historic Clachan Inn, Drymen also boasts the last bank, outdoor equipment shop and well-stocked grocery that walkers will see for several days.

Accommodation

If you want to get a good night's sleep in Milngavie before you start your walk, there are several B&Bs in and around town: these include the long-established **Best Foot Forward** (bestfootforward.eu.com) and **Barloch Guest House** (barlochguesthouse.co.uk) in Strathblane Road, both a few minutes from the start of the walk. The **West Highland Gate Premier Inn** is also not far away on Main Street (visit-lochlomond.com). For campers who like a hot shower in the morning, the best option is **Bankell Farm Campsite** (bankellfarm.co.uk) about 2.5km northeast of Milngavie, clearly signposted off the A81 Strathblane Road.

For most walkers, Drymen marks the end of the first day, but before you reach the village

itself there are two camping options: the **Wishingwell Coffee Shop and Campsite** at Gartness is a good place to get a bite to eat and a hot shower and, further on, **Drymen Camping** at Easter Drumquhassle Farm (drymencamping.co.uk) has wigwam bunkhouses (sleeping six in each) as well as tent pitches. In Drymen the 48-room **Winnock Hotel** (winnockhotel.com) on Drymen's town square and the historic **Buchanan Arms** (buchananarms.co.uk) cater for those who like to rest up in style, otherwise there are plenty of well-established B&Bs scattered in and around town. Among them, **The Old School** (oldschooldrymen.co.uk), **Elmbank** (elmbank-drymen.co.uk) and **Glenalva** (glenalva-drymen.co.uk) are very conveniently sited just off the route as you approach on Stirling Road. The **Clachan Inn** also has rooms (see dellta.org for more B&B options). The late-opening village shop is the best place to stock up on food supplies.

▼ Dumgoyne and Glengoyne Distillery

Drymen to Rowardennan

Distance 24km **Ascent** 560m **Terrain** forest tracks, exposed moorland and one rough climb; easy path along Loch Lomond with many little ups and downs

Those starting the stage from the centre of Drymen have the option of two sneaky shortcuts: by road direct to Balmaha, or northwards up a minor road to straighten out a loop of the official path through the eastern corner of Garadhban Forest, regaining the West Highland Way at a forest car park. The former completely avoids the climb over Conic Hill, which would be a great shame in all but truly grim weather. The latter seems logical, as it's more direct than the standard route, and doesn't miss much. But if shortcuts look like cheating then your day will kick off a little east of Drymen. A long stretch through the mature pine plantations of Garadhban Forest follows: keep an eye open for deer and red squirrels in the gloom on either side. Just before quitting the forest, another sneaky alternative low-level route branches off leftwards – it's inferior, but perhaps worth considering if the weather has really deteriorated since leaving Drymen. It descends to the road at Milton of Buchanan, and then follows this

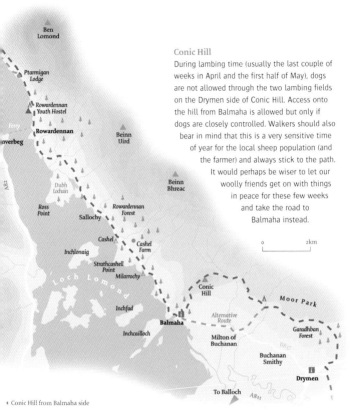

Ben Lomond

Ptarmigan Lodge

Rowardennan Youth Hostel

Rowardennan

Ferry

averbeg

Beinn Uird

Dubh Lochain

Ross Point

Rowardennan Forest

Sallochy

Beinn Bhreac

Cashel

Cashel Farm

Inchlonaig

Strathcashell Point

Milarrochy

Conic Hill

Moor Park

Loch Lomond

Inchfad

Balmaha

Alternative Route

Milton of Buchanan

Garadhban Forest

Inchcailloch

Buchanan Smithy

Drymen

To Balloch

A811

Conic Hill

During lambing time (usually the last couple of weeks in April and the first half of May), dogs are not allowed through the two lambing fields on the Drymen side of Conic Hill. Access onto the hill from Balmaha is allowed but only if dogs are closely controlled. Walkers should also bear in mind that this is a very sensitive time of year for the local sheep population (and the farmer) and always stick to the path. It would perhaps be wiser to let our woolly friends get on with things in peace for these few weeks and take the road to Balmaha instead.

0   2km

◂ Conic Hill from Balmaha side

to rejoin the main route at Balmaha.

After nearly 5km in Garadhban Forest, the main route emerges onto a clear-felled area that soon becomes open moorland. Here is the first chance to look down over the wide island-studded lower reaches of Loch Lomond. In bad weather this stage can be exposed to the elements. Today's only notable climb is onto Conic Hill. The ascent is rough and muddy, and turns into a stream in the rain, but the hard work is repaid with superb views along

21

the length of the loch to the gnarled Arrochar peaks. There's a sense that you've finally crossed the threshold of the Highlands. This is more than just a symbolic gateway. Conic Hill happens to sit on the Highland Boundary Fault, a geological rupture running right across Scotland from Kintyre to Aberdeenshire dividing the Highlands from the Lowlands; a string of islands in Loch Lomond shows its direction. The West Highland Way avoids the very summit of the hill by skirting its upper flanks along a sort of shelf, though the top is only a short detour on an obvious side path and justifies the extra climb on a clear day. The descent is abrupt, and the path in quite a bad state of disrepair. Just before

the final steep drop from Conic Hill there is yet another potential shortcut, worth considering if you've no need to visit the small village of Balmaha: follow a pronounced hummocky ridge running southwest along the line of the Boundary Fault, a very pleasant bit of grassy ridge walking with a last steep descent through woods to the lochside road and West Highland Way 500m north of Balmaha.

The longer official route passes through a fine stand of pines to reach the loch at Balmaha. This might be a good place for a well-earned shandy or, if time isn't pressing, a leisurely afternoon spent nosing a hire boat among the nearby islands. The West Highland Way now follows the east shore for the best part of

30km, and it's immediately clear that the old song didn't lie: Loch Lomond's banks are indeed bonny. It is the largest natural freshwater loch in Scotland, a broad body of water in the south, tapering into a dramatic narrow trench as it cuts northwards between the mountains. Forming some of the most extensive semi-natural native woodland left in Scotland, stands of oak, birch and Scots pine crowd to the waterline, where shingly beaches offer the chance of a secluded skinny dip or a sneaky wild camp (please, no fires). Being so close to the city, Loch Lomond is enjoyed by many thousands of visitors, and can be as packed as a Mediterranean beach resort on summer weekends. This places it on the frontline of a culture clash between nature lovers and those who seem intent on turning their surroundings into a dustbin. The amount of litter scattered along the shore is a national disgrace: those who are upset by this kind of brainless vandalism will feel their anger steadily ebbing as they continue north away from the car parks and the mess.

Just outside Balmaha, the path passes over the little wooded knoll of Craigie Fort for a superb view of the nearby islands. It then wiggles along the shore, sometimes following the road, sometimes deep in the trees. At Sallochy there's a chance to make a detour to an old abandoned village a short uphill walk

Native woodland

The barren treeless landscapes that many associate with the Highlands are not entirely natural. Once the glaciers of the last Ice Age had retreated trees began to colonise the land, and by about 7000 years ago many Highland glens had become densely forested and species rich. Subsequent climate change and human activity gradually depleted Scotland's native woodlands, and today they are scattered and comparatively uncommon. Native woods are no longer widely felled, yet overgrazing by sheep and poorly controlled deer populations (upon which there has been no natural predation since wolves were wiped out) discourages regeneration. In the warm wet west, native woods tend to be made up of oak and birch, while the drier climate further east favours Scots pine. These woods provide ideal habitats for wildlife such as pine martens, red squirrels, capercaillie and wildcats (now extremely rare). In contrast, commercial plantations of alien conifer species make up the overwhelming bulk of Scotland's tree cover; at their worst these are virtual monocultures that do not provide ideal wildlife habitats. The prevailing ethos in Scottish forestry now favours biodiversity and the reintroduction of native tree species, though changes on the ground will be slow to come through.

◂ The island of Inchcailloch from Balmaha Boatyard

off the main route; slowly crumbling as nature reclaims it, this can seem a spooky place as dusk gathers in the trees.

Beyond Sallochy a very pleasant lochside section winds through the oaks and past a car park to a bay overlooked by a field centre owned by Glasgow University. A stiff pull up stone steps then

The Clearances

In common with the rest of the Highlands, the east shore of Loch Lomond and its islands were once farmed and populous. Rural communities thrived on cultivation, livestock grazing and charcoal burning. Today's depopulated landscape is largely the result of the Clearances of the 18th and 19th centuries. The clan system had begun to unravel and, instead of exacting tribute in the age-old custom, clan chieftains became conventional landowners making a living from the rent they charged their tenant farmers, people who'd worked the land for generations. Then economic changes gave the landlords a more profitable option. Over several decades many tenant communities were forcibly evicted, making way for large-scale sheep and cattle farming. Thousands of dispossessed Highlanders emigrated to the New World, never to return. The Clearances remain contentious. Some historians consider them uniquely ignoble, an early form of ethnic cleansing; others, however, place these events in a wider economic context, and point out that such brutality towards the lower social orders was then common throughout the British Isles. Either way, the past is neither forgotten nor totally forgiven. Ruined farmsteads and villages such as Wester Sallochy are a testament to that time.

Looking north up Loch Lomond ▾

takes you to a high point of nearly 100m in Ross Wood. The gradual descent includes some boggy ground and a couple of short boardwalks. Beyond a cottage on the shore the path twists through more idyllic waterside woods, finally meeting the road at the cabins and hotel 1km south of Rowardennan Lodge Youth Hostel.

Accommodation

If you plan to push on from Drymen on your first day and rest up in Balmaha, then there are a few options for you in this pretty (though often very busy) village. The excellent **Oak Tree Inn** (oak-tree-inn.co.uk) makes walkers very welcome and also has bunkhouse accommodation available. Nearby **Passfoot** (passfoot.com) and **Bay Cottage** are gloriously sited B&Bs. Further on from Balmaha,

Milarrochy Bay Campsite is a popular stop with great views and a handy laundry and shop on site. About 3km further on from there, the Forestry Commission's **Cashel Caravan and Campsite** has a snack bar, shop and laundry. This stretch of the walk also passes some B&Bs on the way to Rowardennan, including **Northwood** and **Anchorage Cottage** (anchoragecottage.co.uk) near Sallochy. In Rowardennan, the historic **Rowardennan Hotel** (rowardennanhotel.co.uk) awaits walkers who like a bit of pampering, but most only see the inside of the Clansman Bar before ending their day at **Rowardennan Youth Hostel** (syha.org.uk), a former Victorian hunting lodge five minutes further on with around 75 bunks. Wild camping is also possible (for one night only, no fires) in a clearing provided just past the hostel.

Rowardennan to Inverarnan

Distance 23km **Ascent** 400m **Terrain** forest tracks to start, then a long stage on a twisting lochside path, occasionally rough underfoot and with many little ups and downs. An optional variation provides by far the hardest walk on the West Highland Way

The tramp along the east shore of Loch Lomond north of Rowardennan is generally renowned as the roughest single stage of the entire route. While this isn't necessarily saying much, it's true that the path's countless little ups, downs and wiggles make for harder work than might be appreciated looking at a map; by day's end your legs will feel the cumulative effect. But with perspiration comes inspiration. Swathes of native woodland, a peaceful lochside setting and stirring mountain views make this arguably the most beautiful stretch of any British long-distance footpath – unless

that is you happen not to be a fan of trees, rocks and water (if so, our commiserations). It is particularly memorable in autumn and spring. If you're out early and first on the trail, there's a good chance of spotting wildlife including shaggy feral goats – you'll smell them before they smell you.

From the leafy car park and National Park info centre, take the forest track past a gravel beach, the entrance to Rowardennan Lodge Youth Hostel and some cottages. The track then follows the loch shore at the foot of Ben Lomond, and shortly begins to climb above Ptarmigan Lodge, the roof of which can just be seen through the trees. Just beyond the lodge, the route splits into two strands for several kilometres. We'll be shamelessly cheesy and call them the High Road and the Low Road.

The High Road The preferred option for

◄ Near the Inversnaid boathouse

most walkers – particularly the heavily laden – this is the obvious quick way to go, direct and to the point. Simply stay on the 4WD track through thick woods, ignoring any side turnings. After the first big climb, it is gentle walking with few ups and downs. Occasionally it's possible to catch a glimpse of the loch far below. Some 4km of fairly uniform terrain, at one point passing a steep little crag hidden in the trees, brings you to a reasonably taxing descent, beyond which the track shrinks to a woodland path.

The Low Road Neither the north nor the south ends of this variant are signposted – you have to really want it. Don't infer from the fact that it is described here that this path is suitable for everyone. It is far more strenuous than the High Road, or indeed any other stretch of the West Highland Way - a very tiring way to start what is in any case a fairly hard day. Yet this is a deeply satisfying place to walk. It has an adventurous feel, involving plenty of mud, clambering around fallen trees, many steep little climbs and several scrambly bits above deep cold water. Anyone who has 'walked' in the Rwenzori or New Guinea will feel at home. Payback for the graft is the unspoilt surroundings of mossy woodland and rocky shore. After a considerable stretch of lochside jungle bashing the path climbs away from the water through thick pine woods, passing secluded Rowchoish Bothy. This is a top-spec shelter with sophisticated

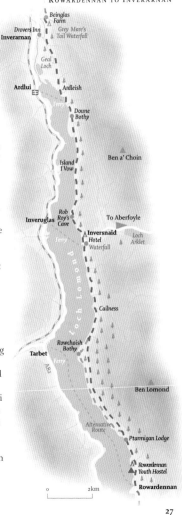

Beinglas Farm
Drovers Inn
Inverarnan
Grey Mare's Tail Waterfall
Geal Loch
Ardlui
Ardleish
Doune Bothy
Ben a' Choin
Island I Vow
Rob Roy's Cave
Inveruglas
To Aberfoyle
Inversnaid Hotel
Waterfall
Loch Arklet
Loch Lomond
Cailness
Rowchoish Bothy
Tarbet
Ben Lomond
Alternative Route
Ptarmigan Lodge
Rowardennan Youth Hostel
Rowardennan

0   2km

27

Bothies

The bothy is a longstanding Scottish mountain institution. Scattered throughout the hills, these rough remote shelters provide a free roof (and sometimes little more) for anyone who happens to drop by. Facilities tend to be on the spartan side, closer to indoor camping than the sort of luxurious wardened mountain hotels with which continental visitors might be more familiar. Those planning on using a bothy will need a sleeping bag, mat and stove. Many are maintained by volunteers from the Mountain Bothies Association (MBA), a charity that looks after more than 100 such shelters. Bothy locations are not generally advertised, partly to prevent vandalism and overuse. Among those in the know, there's a sense of being in an exclusive club. Here's a little secret: there are two bothies between Rowardennan and Inverarnan. They can be very busy during summer weekends. Please follow the 'bothy code' as listed in MBA-maintained huts – it's all common sense stuff.

mod cons such as a sleeping platform and a functioning fireplace. With its spooky Hansel and Gretel setting, it makes an atmospheric place to spend the night. Beyond Rowchoish the path rejoins the main track, at the point just before it becomes a path.

Now continue downhill on the path to regain the loch shore not far from the private cottage at Cailness. For most of the rest of the day, the path is never far from the water, threading a course through thriving woodland, backed by steep rocky slopes. You'll soon lose count of the idyllic little gravel beaches and grassy camping spots: on a hot day thoughts of swimming are hard to resist, though the water is always glacial. A bridge over a sizeable waterfall brings you to Inversnaid Hotel, incongruously vast and ugly for

such a gorgeous setting. It's worth descending to the jetty to see the waterfall from beneath in its full glory. The hotel is accessible from the east by a minor dead-end road, and from the west by a privately-run boat service across the loch from Inveruglas.

Beyond the hotel and its coach party crowds you're soon re-immersed in unspoilt beauty. Rob Roy's Cave is well worth a look if you enjoy slithering over rocks. The path passes under a steep rock outcrop; the cave is hidden among a jumble of huge boulders below, and the best way to it is signed. It's more of a tight, muddy squeeze between house-sized blocks than a majestic cavern. Somebody has still seen fit to write CAVE in big white letters beside its upper entrance, presumably for the benefit of boat-borne visitors.

Continue past a meadow at Pollochro, beyond which the path becomes rougher and stonier for a while. Then cross open ground backing a small bay, where the path briefly peels from the shore to climb over a wooded knoll. Descend to Doune, the second bothy en route. It's not exactly The Ritz, but it does keep rain and midges at bay. Just beyond Doune, the path passes a request ferry stop – raise a marker and they'll come across and pick you up (in season). The West Highland Way then quits the lochside for good, climbing through a mini glen before

descending gradually among scattered woods to Beinglas Farm, a pleasant campsite and a good base for climbing nearby Beinn Chabhair (*see detour p54*) for those with excess energy. The Drovers Inn – 'Scottish Pub of the Year 1705' – at Inverarnan is just a short walk down a track and along the A82.

Accommodation

If you don't fancy the bothies, but are thinking of splitting this section, then the functional **Inversnaid Hotel**, which caters primarily for coach tours who arrive via the winding road from Aberfoyle, also does limited B&B for walkers. There are also a couple of clearings five minutes on from the hotel where you can strike **camp** (for one night only). If you have had a longer trek to Inverarnan, however, then the hot showers at **Beinglas Campsite** (beinglascampsite.co.uk), situated right on the Way, will make it all seem worthwhile. The site has wigwam-style bunkhouses (sleeping four), a laundry, a bar and restaurant and a good little shop with most things a tired walker might need. Nearby, the equally idyllic **Clisham** (clishamcottage.com) and **Rose Cottage** also offer B&B, as does the always entertaining **Drovers Inn** (thedroversinn.co.uk).

◄ Doune Bothy

Inverarnan to Crianlarich

Distance 9.5km **Ascent** 230m **Terrain** easy tracks and a very gradual ascent

This modest stage could readily be run into the following one for a more stretching day, or perhaps spiced up with an ascent of Beinn Chabhair and/or An Caisteal (*see p54*): alternatively finish early and enjoy an afternoon at the pub in Crianlarich.

From the campsite follow a gravel track north along Glen Falloch, mirroring the course of the River Falloch through a mix of open woodland and pasture. The famous Falls of Falloch are a series of cascades and rapids, best seen when the surrounding trees aren't in full leaf. They make a great excuse to stop for a break. The West Highland Way now follows the course of a pylon line for a few kilometres, accompanied by the road and railway that share the bottom of the glen – despite

these, the walking is pleasant. Beyond the farm buildings at Derrydaroch, cross the river. On the other bank is a scattered remnant of old Caledonian pine wood, one of the few to be seen on the West Highland Way. The path soon ducks through a 'sheep creep', a head-crackingly low underpass beneath the railway; it then follows a very short stretch of disused tarmac road before passing under the A82. As Glen Falloch widens, climb gradually away from the road on a stretch of track that started life as a military road.

The track takes you through a nice open stretch, with views of some big peaks – Cruach Ardrain, Ben More and Stob Binnein. A short distance beyond Keilator Farm, climb into a forestry plantation.

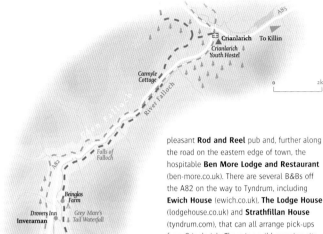

Beyond a gate in a deer fence is the right-hand turn-off for Crianlarich, a quick descent through woods that reaches the village outskirts just opposite the railway station. Close to several striking mountains, Crianlarich is the hillwalking capital of the Southern Highlands. With a range of facilities and transport links it makes a good base for a peak-bagging trip.

Accommodation

With around 70 bunks usually available, **Crianlarich Youth Hostel** (crianlarich youthhostel.org.uk) is a popular stop and many walkers stay a day longer to recover from the tough Loch Lomond section. There are also a few B&Bs in the village, including **Glenardran House** (glenardran.co.uk), well-situated near the

pleasant **Rod and Reel** pub and, further along the road on the eastern edge of town, the hospitable **Ben More Lodge and Restaurant** (ben-more.co.uk). There are several B&Bs off the A82 on the way to Tyndrum, including **Ewich House** (ewich.co.uk), **The Lodge House** (lodgehouse.co.uk) and **Strathfillan House** (tyndrum.com), that can all arrange pick-ups from Crianlarich. There is a wild camping site where the Way crosses the River Fillan, but the bunkhouses at **Strathfillan Wigwam Village** (wigwamholidays.com/strathfillan) at Auchtertyre Farm are worth pushing on for. If Tyndrum itself is your destination for the night, then the excellent **By the Way Hostel and Campsite** (tyndrumbytheway.com) is well-situated – as the name suggests – and can accommodate a lot of walkers in their campsite, trekker huts and hostel. There are also a few B&B options around, including **Dalkell Cottage** (dalkell.com) and **Glengarry House** (glengarryhouse.com), as well as the **Invervey Hotel** (inverveyhotel.co.uk) next door to the unmissable **Green Welly Stop**. Supplies for the next day's walking can be bought here or at **Brodies Mini-Market** at the north end of Tyndrum. Also well worth a mention as the best place in the village to eat is the friendly and affordable **Real Food Café**.

Crianlarich to Bridge of Orchy

Distance 21km **Ascent** 390m
Terrain clear, well-drained paths and gravel
tracks throughout – very trainer friendly.
A couple of modest ascents

Regain the West Highland Way in the
forested hills above the village. A gravelly
footpath weaves through the trees for
several kilometres, a series of wiggly ups
and downs with only occasional views

over Strath Fillan to the undulating
mountain skyline above Crianlarich.
The dense pines muffle any noise from
the distant road, creating a feeling of
enclosed peace. After reaching a high
point at about 360m the West Highland
Way gradually descends to the glen,
passing under the railway before crossing
the A82 (caution – fast-moving traffic).
It then crosses a bridge over the broad

Drove roads

These ancient tracks crisscross Britain and were originally used to drive vast herds of cattle to
distant markets in the days before factory farming and refrigerated HGVs. Cows were a staple of the
old Highland economy, with a chieftain's wealth measured by his head of cattle. As well as being
killed for meat, live cattle could be bled, the blood then mixed with oatmeal to create a tasty black
pudding-style snack. Highland cattle were a major export for the area, and were sold in large
numbers at annual lowland markets. The drovers that got them there were skilled and respected
men. The key on a drove was striking the right pace – walk too slow and you'd miss the market, but
travel too fast and the cattle would lose weight, and thus value. Tyndrum was once a welcome stop-
over for drovers on the way down from the Highland glens, though most footsore travellers who pass
this way nowadays prefer their coos medium rare with chips.

　　　　　　　　　　　　　　　　　▲ Highland cattle in Strath Fillan

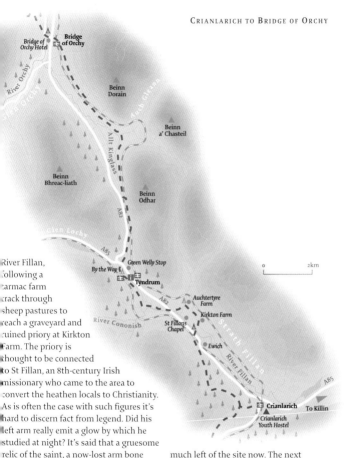

River Fillan, following a tarmac farm track through sheep pastures to reach a graveyard and ruined priory at Kirkton Farm. The priory is thought to be connected to St Fillan, an 8th-century Irish missionary who came to the area to convert the heathen locals to Christianity. As is often the case with such figures it's hard to discern fact from legend. Did his left arm really emit a glow by which he studied at night? It's said that a gruesome relic of the saint, a now-lost arm bone held in a silver casket, was borne into battle at Bannockburn at the request of Robert the Bruce. Perhaps he was seeking to win by force of arms. Whatever Fillan got up to in life or afterwards, there's not much left of the site now. The next farm is Auchtertyre, which offers camping, wigwam accommodation and a small shop. Extensive moraines in this part of Strath Fillan are a relic of Scotland's glacial past.

Back on the west side of the A82, swimming fans get a chance to let it all hang out at a cascade and deep clear pool in the River Cononish, beneath an old stone bridge. Legend maintains that a plunge in the river hereabouts can cure insanity, thanks to the influence of the good Irish evangelist. Perhaps you'd have to be mad in the first place to want to leap into a Highland river? Go on, you know it makes sense.

Soon after comes Tyndrum Community Woodland, an area of re-planted native trees covering a hillocky patch of old moraines: it will be very nice in a couple of decades, when the trees have grown up. Half glimpsed up the side valley of the River Cononish is the twin-peaked Ben Lui, one of the most majestic sights in the Southern Highlands – particularly when snow covered. Its ascent from here is a full

day round-trip via the scrambly ridges enclosing Coire Gaothach (not suited to beginners) (*see detour p56*). Beyond some old lead mine workings, a riverside section through mature pines leads to Tyndrum, where shops, accommodation and a really good café can be found.

Climb gently out of the village, now back on the course of the old military road. The one drawback of this section is that the path is squeezed into a narrow pass alongside the A82 and the railway line. But though this is the major transport artery between Scotland's largest city and the West Highlands, traffic noise rarely seems intrusive. Above a water treatment works the little gorge of the Crom Allt contains several enticing plunge pools, though getting to them safely could be an issue.

Pass beneath the grassy shapeless

▲ Beinn Dorain and Beinn O

splodge of Beinn Odhar (*see detour p58*), with an unfolding view of Beinn Dorain ahead (*see detour p60*). From this angle its steep prow is a graceful cone – Scotland's answer to Fuji-san. Go under the railway line and descend the track to a floodplain where Highland cows can often be seen grazing. This is a peaceful corner, the road now some distance away. Beyond the farm buildings, the West Highland Way continues for several kilometres under the great green uniform sweep of Beinn Dorain's western flank, crossing and re-crossing the railway to eventually reach Bridge of Orchy. It is a one-horse kind of place, only it seems the horse has left town in search of excitement. Though this huddle of houses is too small to be called a village it is a good place to stop for the night.

Accommodation

Railway buffs arriving in Bridge of Orchy will especially love the **West Highland Way Sleeper** (westhighlandwaysleeper.co.uk), a two-roomed hostel housed in the original West Highland Line station. The bunkhouse belonging to the **Bridge of Orchy Hotel** (scottish-selection.co.uk) is another option unless you want to splash out on a bit more luxury in the hotel itself. Hardier souls can also make use of the **free campsite** across the bridge, although the local midges can be fearsome. Thankfully the hotel's excellent **Caley Bar** is not far away. If you want to go a bit further before stopping for the night, then the historic **Inveroran Hotel** at the end of peaceful Loch Tulla offers B&B and provides a **free campsite** for walkers who might also want to get comfortable in the **Walkers Bar** (enter round the back).

Tyndrum's mines

For nearly two hundred years from the mid-18th century, lead ore was mined in the mountains surrounding Tyndrum. The workings are still visible, especially on the slopes west of the village. The nearby Cononish goldmine has been inactive for decades, though it's thought to have several years' worth of ore. Its owners hope to start commercial mining in the near future: it'll never be a huge operation, but Scottish gold is amongst the most expensive in the world because of its rarity. This mini Highland Klondike attracts occasional amateur panning enthusiasts too, and though the chances of tapping a rich vein are pretty low one determined repeat visitor has managed to glean enough gold for his wife's wedding ring – and they say romance is dead. Keep your eyes skinned when crossing streams, and be ready to stake a claim.

Bridge of Orchy to Kingshouse

Distance 19km **Ascent** 520m **Terrain** paths, gravel tracks and even some tarmac. In places, the surroundings are comparatively remote and exposed to bad weather

This is a fairly tough stage with a couple of appreciable climbs. Crossing a corner of Rannoch Moor beneath the wild Black Mount range, the surroundings are perhaps the most remote and exciting of the whole walk, a dun-coloured expanse of heather, water and nothingness. There is very little shelter along the way, making life potentially unpleasant (or worse) in foul conditions; and foul is, arguably, the default position for Rannoch Moor weather. But on a clear day you're in for a rare treat.

Start on the west bank of the River Orchy, with a short climb through pine plantations, sometimes soggy underfoot. Beyond the woods the path zigzags over the broad shoulder of Màm Carraigh, cairns marking the high point and a chance to admire the view of things to come – beautiful Loch Tulla, Rannoch Moor and the bold peaks of the Black Mount (*see detour p64*). Descend to the minor road at Inveroran Hotel, the last (and only) refreshment stop all day. Loch Tulla is fringed with healthy woodland of native Scots pine, ecologically richer and much prettier than the nearby plantations of alien evergreens. Follow the road past a little cottage, looping the head of the loch to reach the houses at Forest Lodge.

◄ Loch Tulla

King's House Hotel

Buachaille Etive Mor

River Etive

Blackrock Cottage

White Corries

Meall a' Bhuiridh

Ba Cottage (ruin)

Ba Bridge

River Ba

Black Mount

Stob a' Choire Odhair

Beinn Toaig

Victoria Bridge

Inveroran Hotel

Abhainn Shira

Loch Tulla

Bridge of Orchy Hotel

Bridge of Orchy

0   2km

Military roads

The 18th century was a time of religious and political strife, a power struggle of Catholic versus Protestant, Tory versus Whig, in which the British throne was contested between the houses of Stuart and Hanover. Aided by the French, the Jacobite uprisings of 1715 and 1745 sought to restore a Stuart to the throne. Their final decisive defeat came at Culloden in 1746. Though the Jacobite cause had had supporters throughout the British Isles, it's no accident that the bulk of its fighters came from the Highlands. Here the ancient patriarchal clan system still held sway, a feudal (and feuding) way of life in which people were bound by strong ties of loyalty to their chieftains. Each chieftain could, in effect, call on a small army of clansmen. The area was inaccessible, very remote from central control, and so effectively ungovernable. Think modern Afghanistan, with kilts. To aid the movement of troops and supplies, government forces set about building a network of military roads and forts – at first in direct response to the Jacobite threat, and then later to ensure that the area remained subdued. In all, nearly 2000km of roads were built in Scotland linking sites of strategic importance. Inns built along the roads – King's Houses like the one in Glencoe – provided food, drink and shelter for the road-builders.

The old road now continues as a track of unsurfaced cobbles, climbing gradually beside more woods to reach the high desolate country on the western fringes of Rannoch Moor.

Passing a couple of lonely forestry plantations at the foot of Beinn Toaig, the track descends slightly into the mouth of

37

Coireach a' Bà, a huge and magnificent corrie system encircled by the towering Black Mount peaks. The corrie rims are often heavily corniced late into spring. Pass a small loch to reach Bà Bridge, halfway point between Inveroran and the

King's House, and as isolated a spot as any on the West Highland Way. Care is needed if you're tempted by the little crystal clear pools here, as the flow is quite powerful.

After a gentle climb to a saddle at 450m, the A82 is visible below. The track

Glencoe ski centre

Scotland's commercial downhill skiing industry started here in Glencoe over 40 years ago. It is now one of five Scottish ski centres, all pretty small by international standards. Loyal devotees consider Glencoe to have some of the best skiing in Scotland, and in good conditions they probably have a point. OK, so it's not Val d'Isere, but those unfamiliar with it might be surprised to learn how good Scottish skiing can be. Of course it can also be dreadful, with irregular unpredictable snowfall, brutal weather, frequent thaws and a surface of ice, slush and gravel. But pick a sunny day with a fresh dump of white stuff and you'll be in downhill heaven, with the added advantages of few crowds and no posers. How often can you say that about the Alps?

descends below Meall a' Bhùiridh, home of the Glencoe Mountain Resort, Scotland's original ski centre. It reaches the ski road at the much-photographed Blackrock Cottage, a private climbers' club hut. Ahead, the huge squat form of Buachaille Etive Mor begins to dominate your attention. Now reach and cross the main road, and follow the onward track to the King's House Hotel.

Accommodation

Always popular with hikers and climbers, the **King's House Hotel** (kingy.com) is the only place to get a meal, a pint and a soft bed on this part of the Way before Kinlochleven.

You can also pitch your tent in the area provided over the bridge but be aware that the river can rise quickly in the night and that the hotel won't open up their loos in the morning no matter how hard you knock! Alternatively, you could catch a bus along the A82 towards the village of Glencoe and get off at the famed **Clachaig Inn** (clachaig.com) and take a room there – unless your name is Campbell that is. Further up the minor road from the 'Clach', you can also pitch your tent at the easygoing **Red Squirrel Campsite** (redsquirrelcampsite.com). The idyllic **Glencoe Youth Hostel** (syha.org.uk) and the **Glencoe Independent Hostel** (glencoehostel.co.uk) are also not far along the same road.

▾ Blackrock Cottage and 'The Buachaille'

Kingshouse to Kinlochleven

Distance 14.5km **Ascent** 420m **Terrain** brief butch climb with some rough rubbly stretches leads to the route's windswept high point, then a finish on Landrover tracks

This may be a short stage, but it is also sharp. It includes the most significant ascent on the entire West Highland Way, over a high pass at 550m via the ominous-sounding Devil's Staircase. On a day of hellish weather this uphill switchback might seem an infernal purgatory, but if you're fit and fresh and the sun is shining it's more like heaven, with views to die for.

Cross the bridge behind the King's House and turn left to follow an old road running roughly parallel to the A82. Across the glen Buachaille Etive Mor sprouts out of the moor, a great mass of rock buttresses and deep gullies building to a crescendo on a high spearhead peak. Whether brooding menacingly under dank clouds or raising glistening ice-crusted battlements into a blue sky, this is one of the most distinctive mountains in Scotland (hence the world). Before the road meets the A82 the West Highland Way branches off rightwards, continuing under Beinn a' Chrulaiste to reach the car park at Altnafeadh. The path now quits the roadside to climb the heathery slope leading to the Devil's Staircase, a series of zigzags that climb up to the pass. The top is crowned by cairns. Behind you are fantastic views over the eastern reaches of Glencoe and the wild wastes of Rannoch Moor, but the northward panorama is just as inspiring: the long ribbon of

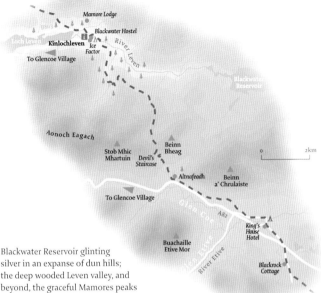

Blackwater Reservoir glinting silver in an expanse of dun hills; the deep wooded Leven valley, and beyond, the graceful Mamores peaks crowding the horizon. From the cairns it is possible to make a quick detour to either of the small summits flanking the pass, west to Stob Mhic Mhartuin or east to Beinn Bheag.

The West Highland Way now drops into the head of a shallow glen, a remote secluded spot and not the best place to twist an ankle. It then rounds a shoulder to begin the descent towards Kinlochleven, which is soon visible far below, a cluster of houses nestled at the mouth of the Leven valley. Loch Leven is a classic sea loch, a thin fjord-like sliver of

The Devil's Staircase

So named by the soldiers who climbed up here daily in the 1750s to build Major Caulfield's military road through to Kinlochleven, the Devil's Staircase earned even greater infamy during the construction of the Blackwater Dam in the early 1900s. On wages day, after an evening spent drinking in the King's House, the weary labourers would face a long stagger back to camp and inevitably, on wild winter nights, the devil would frequently 'claim his own'.

tidal water squeezed between steep-sided mountains. The open sea is many miles away, south of Oban. As it loses height the path becomes rough and rubbly.

There is another series of zigzags in descent, much like the Devil's Staircase, but soon the path joins a vehicle track at some buildings that mark the top of the

Blackwater Dam building

Kinlochleven was once a thriving industrial centre, known locally as Electric Village. The town grew up in the early 1900s, built by the British Aluminium Company to house workers for the smelter which in its heyday employed up to 800 people. Aluminium smelting demands an enormous electric charge, here generated by hydro turbines fed by water from the Blackwater Reservoir several kilometres up-valley. Pipelines still carry vast volumes of water into town, though the smelter closed several years ago. The Blackwater Dam and its associated concrete aqueducts and steel pipelines (nearly 25km in all) represent the end of an era, as the last monumental engineering project to be carried out by navvies. Popular mythology has it that navvies, migrant labourers mainly from Ireland, more or less built the British Empire through the sweat of their brows. While there's an element of truth in this, it is easy to over-romanticise the past. Living in squalor and semi-lawlessness, the average Blackwater navvy would have drunk and fought as hard as he worked, enduring harsh and dangerous conditions high in the hills for a relative pittance. Many were injured or killed at work and beneath the dam is a graveyard for those who died in its construction, a bleak reminder of the price ordinary people paid building Britain's industry and infrastructure.

impressive Alcan works pipeline.

The vehicle track is very stony and steep at first, and takes a far from direct route. By this stage in the day you may feel a little footsore, but the surrounding birch woods are a pleasant distraction. Because for most of the last century the people of Kinlochleven were too busy making aluminium to bother with large-scale sheep farming, the area's native woodlands have had a chance to regenerate. Every glen on the west coast was once similarly forested, and it is sadly telling that Kinlochleven's patchy woods are now worthy of note for their relative extent.

After wandering around the hillsides for a while the track eventually deigns to meet the pipeline, then descends to the works on the edge of town. Heavy industry is a thing of the past here: these days the old works buildings house the award-winning Atlas Brewery and the world's largest artificial ice climbing wall, the Ice Factor, as the community that was built on aluminium seeks to reinvent itself in a post-industrial age. Facilities at Kinlochleven include a bank, post office, grocery shops, bunkhouse and B&Bs. For the vertically inclined, the Ice Factor is well worth a visit, and houses a conventional climbing wall alongside its giant freezer.

Accommodation

As you would expect of the home to the awesome **Ice Factor** (ice-factor.co.uk) and the excellent **Atlas Brewery** (atlasbrewery.com), the little town of Kinlochleven makes walkers feel very welcome. The well-run **Blackwater Hostel and Campsite** (blackwaterhostel.co.uk), just past the end of the water pipes as you come down the hill, has 40 beds and 30 pitches and they have another smaller overflow hostel not far away. Further on and over the bridge, the campsite at the **MacDonald Hotel** (macdonaldhotel.co.uk) has great views down Loch Leven and nine cosy four-bunk cabins available. There is also no shortage of B&B accommodation around – the **Tailrace Inn** (tailraceinn.co.uk), **Tigh na Cheo** (tigh-na-cheo.co.uk) and **Edencoille Guest House** (kinlochlevenbedandbreakfast.co.uk) – are all easy to find. A bit more unusual is the wonderfully grand **Mamore Lodge Hotel** (mamorelodgehotel.co.uk), a former hunting lodge situated high above Kinlochleven on the lower slopes of Am Bodach. It's a bit of a climb to get to, but the welcoming bar, period decor and stunning views help soothe the pain.

Kinlochleven to Fort William

Distance 22.5km **Ascent** 730m
Terrain a notable hill stage through a wild
mountain pass, sometimes rough and wet
underfoot; then easy forest paths and tracks
for a long lingering finish

A hard grind from sea level gets the blood
pumping first thing – this is arguably the
most strenuous climb on the entire route.
Walk out of town along the north loop of
the minor road that circles Loch Leven:
the path starts just opposite a school.
It is a steep ascent through scattered
birch woods, with views back down to
Kinlochleven in its shady hollow and over
the fjord-like ribbon of Loch Leven to the
jagged Aonach Eagach ridge, a classic
Scottish scramble. Zigzag strenuously
uphill to eventually reach a more level
track on about the 240m contour. This is a

continuation of the old military road that
you've been following on and off for
several days. It now leads through the
well named Lairig Mòr, or Big Pass.

Passing above the wooded gorge of the
Allt Nathrach, the track climbs gradually
towards its high point at about 380m.
Cutting between some little-frequented
700m peaks and the magnificent Mamores
range, Lairig Mòr is the epitome of a
Highland pass – bleak, windswept and
remote. At such close quarters it's hard to
appreciate the full splendour of the
Mamores, graceful pointed summits
slung with narrow ridges that provide
some of the best hillwalking in Scotland.
For the upwardly mobile, a day-long
round trip from Kinlochleven to some of
the summits comes highly recommended
(*see detour p72*). Other than the doubtful

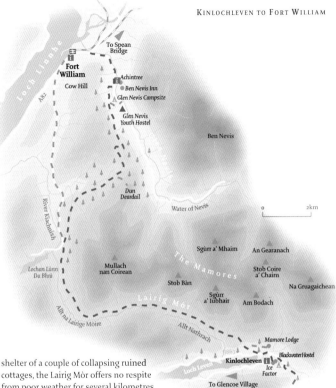

To Spean Bridge

Fort William

Achintree

Cow Hill

Ben Nevis Inn

Glen Nevis Campsite

Glen Nevis Youth Hostel

Ben Nevis

River Kiachnish

Dun Deardail

Water of Nevis

0   2km

Sgùrr a' Mhaim

An Gearanach

Mullach nan Coirean

The Mamores

Stob Coire a' Chairn

Lochan Lùnn Da Bhrà

Stob Bàn

Na Gruagaichean

Sgùrr a' Iubhair

Am Bodach

Lairig Mòr

Allt na Lairige Mòire

Allt Nathrach

Mamore Lodge

Blackwater Hostel

Kinlochleven

Ice Factor

To Glencoe Village

shelter of a couple of collapsing ruined cottages, the Lairig Mòr offers no respite from poor weather for several kilometres, so keep your fingers crossed for sunshine.

Beyond the pass, the West Highland Way rounds the western flanks of the Mamores and soon enters an extensive area of pine plantations, setting the theme for the rest of the walk. After a brief flirtation with a minor road (a more direct route into Fort William, incidentally) the path follows a wiggly series of little ups and downs through the

trees, making, gradually, towards Glen Nevis. Ahead, you'll have an unfolding view of the mighty Ben Nevis in all its lumpen enormity. Only the southwest aspect of the mountain is visible from here: though it is the flank favoured by the only easy path to the summit, it is by far the least attractive side to an

◂ Loch Leven with the Pap of Glencoe on the left

45

otherwise mighty mountain. Through a sort of Jekyll and Hyde split personality, the northern cliffs form the most impressive piece of mountain architecture in Britain. Most walkers barely even realise they exist.

The path eventually emerges from the densest of the pines, descending into Glen Nevis on a long series of forest tracks. If you're staying at Glen Nevis Youth Hostel or the nearby campsite it pays to quit the West Highland Way early, turning hard right on a side track leading to the road in the valley bottom. The official route brings you to the same road about 1km further north. The end is now very much in sight –

The Ben

With its toes in the sea and its head in the clouds (more often than not), the vast hulk of Ben Nevis dominates its surroundings. It has a split personality, an easy rounded flank contrasting with the dramatic craggy north face. Strollers on the ever-popular Tourist Track might be unaware of the mountain's darker side, and have no idea that there's more to 'The Ben' than walking, but it is also a magnet for climbers from around the world. Its altitude combines with moist sea air to build some of the best ice climbing conditions on the planet – in a good winter, that is. The deepest gullies can hold snow long into summer. It used to be said that the summit was only a couple of hundred metres shy of permanent glaciation, and while climate change might have undermined this theory it does still suggest that this is a place to treat with respect. The Ben is a harsh mountain, subject to extreme and changeable weather in every season. The ascent may start at balmy sea level, yet it reaches high into a realm of wind, rain, ice and rock. Mountain Rescue volunteers are routinely called to search for poorly-equipped walkers, and fatalities do occur. Wild land conservation society the John Muir Trust own large tracts of Ben Nevis, managing the land in partnership with other agencies to make sure it is kept unspoilt.

◄ Ben Nevis from the other side of Glen Nevis

all that remains is a tramp along the pavement into Fort William, where the West Highland Way terminates at a roundabout, of all things. From here the town centre is just 1km away. The attraction of this busy local hub is mainly in its setting. At first glance Fort William isn't the most genteel place to finish a walk, but the town does have a certain distinctive charm and character, and is worth a stay in its own right. As the self-styled Outdoor Capital of the UK the Lochaber area could keep you happy for weeks if you're that way inclined, with world-class climbing, hillwalking, mountain biking and watersports all on the doorstep.

On the final leg down Glen Nevis, the sense of serenity that the mountains bring begins to fall away as you re-enter the bustle of normal life. Fort William is well-served by public transport, and you could be back in Glasgow in a few hours. All good things must come to an end, they say. But the town is also the starting point for other long-distance walks. Perhaps you'll get the urge to continue along the Great Glen Way to Inverness; or maybe you'd prefer the unofficial Cape Wrath Trail, one of the most challenging wild walks in

Europe? The West Highland Way may have given you blisters, and an irresistible desire to find a B&B with a proper bath; it should also leave you wanting more.

Accommodation

Fort William is packed with B&Bs, small hotels and budget backpacker hostels which fill up quickly in the summer months. If you prefer things a bit more relaxed, however, there are several very good options in Glen Nevis. If you took the early track down to the glen then the always popular **Glen Nevis Youth Hostel** (glennevishostel.co.uk) is just past the very good Café Beag to your right and the sprawling **Glen Nevis Campsite** (glen-nevis.co.uk) entrance is to your left. Further along the road heading towards town and over the river is **Achintee Farm** (achinteefarm.com), which offers hostel and B&B accommodation, and the characterful **Ben Nevis Inn and Bunkhouse** (bennevisinn.co.uk), easily the best place in the glen to enjoy a pint (and often live music) after finishing the Way or climbing the very nearby Ben Nevis. If you would rather head for the bright lights, then on the way are the pleasant **Ben Nevis** (bennevisguesthouse.com) and **Corrie Duff** (corrieduff.co.uk) guesthouses and, further on, the **Nevis Bank Hotel** (nevisbankhotel.co.uk) is next to the roundabout that marks the official end of the route. Further into Fort William, **Fort William Backpackers** (fortwilliambackpackers.com) on Alma Road and the **Bank St Lodge Bunkhouse** (bankstreetlodge.co.uk) are popular and affordable places to bunk down for the night.

WELCOME TO FORT WILLIAM

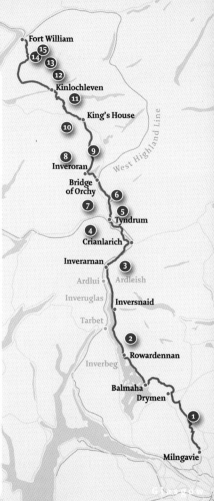

For most people, just finishing the West Highland Way itself is hard work enough. Yet detours from the route offer new perspectives on the country it passes through, and can really enliven the walk. Every day spent on the Way brings you close to an appealing hill or three. From the little rocky cone of Dumgoyne in the south to the massive bulk of Ben Nevis dominating the northern end of the trail, these are some of the most distinctive summits in Scotland. Even the easiest hill detours take you to another level, a world of challenge and beauty far above the busy lower glens. This selection of trips covers many of the obvious trailside peaks and others less well known but equally worthwhile. Most require at least half a day to complete, though some are much shorter. Key low-level trips are also described, for days when the weather or your legs aren't up to scratch.

48

Detours along the Way

Please be aware that the mountain routes described here are significantly
more demanding than anything to be found on the West Highland Way itself,
and are best suited to properly equipped and experienced walkers.

Dumgoyne over Strath Blane

Dumgoyne (427m) **Distance** 3.5km
Ascent 400m **Terrain** clear well-drained path,
if quite steep **Time** 2 hours
Map OS Landranger 64 or 57

Small, but packing quite a punch,
Dumgoyne's craggy cone lords it over the
valley of Strath Blane. It is one of the
most recognisable summits on the course
of the West Highland Way, visible for
much of the walk's first stage. For anyone
with excess energy, the short, sharp
ascent to its summit is a must. Sweeping
from Glasgow's high rises to the islands
of Loch Lomond and the low ridge of
Conic Hill backed by Highland peaks

– on a clear day the view can be quite
a revelation. It offers a sense of your
place in the world – well, the West
Highland Way, at any rate – both where
you've just been, and where you'll soon
be going. Toilers down on the main
path don't get to see things in such
revealing perspective.

From the A81 immediately north of
the distillery, a track runs uphill past a
group of cottages. Stay with it as it curves
through some woods, turning off at a gate
just before the last house up on its own in
the trees. Now follow a path across a
meadow, making a beeline for the squat
form of Dumgoyne. Beyond a double stile,

ttack the hill direct.
series of steps have
een worn up the steep
grass slope, but for a
small hillock it is still
surprisingly hard
work. At about
half height, a path
uts right over a
houlder before
limbing through
ocky hummocks:
his is the gentlest
vay to the top. From
he summit, those in the
know might be able to
make out the Isle of Arran's
haracteristic toothed
skyline, and perhaps even the
knobble of Ailsa Craig, a little
island halfway to Ireland. Descend
he way you came.

Whisky

Whisky is Scotland's national spirit, a drink of strength, complexity and almost limitless subtle
variety; much like the Scots themselves. As every tour guide knows, the name derives from the Gaelic
uisge beatha, or the water of life, which seems ironic given that too much of it could have the opposite
effect. The basic process starts with mashing up malted barley and water. This slop is then fermented
and distilled before the final and perhaps most crucial stage, maturation in fragrant old wooden
casks. What the casks once contained (bourbon or sherry, typically) and where and how long they
stand have a decisive influence on the flavour of the finished product. Single malt is the real deal,
the carefully crafted product of a single distillery; blends are usually (though not always) cheaper and
inferior. No two distilleries or even vintages are ever exactly alike. As with wine, single malts are
grouped by region: Lowland, Highland, Speyside, Campbeltown and Islay, though this is only a very
broad guide to typical characteristics. The Glengoyne is a subtle Highland malt, made with air-dried
barley rather than peat-smoked, and has been distilled here continuously since 1833.

◄ Loch Lomond from the top of Dumgoyne

Ben Lomond by the Ptarmigan

Ben Lomond (974m) **Distance** 9.5km
Ascent 1040m **Terrain** fairly steep in parts,
but clear paths throughout **Time** 4 hours 30
Map OS Landranger 56

The most southerly Munro, Ben Lomond
is one of Scotland's most popular peaks –
and rightly so, being easily accessed and
very attractive. Ben Lomond dominates
the middle reaches of Loch Lomond:
because it sits in a commanding position
near the boundary between Highland
and Lowland, it offers sensational views
over both. The normal there-and-back
route from Rowardennan car park is the
hillwalker's equivalent of a motorway,
busy almost every day of the year. Of
various possible routes of ascent, the
comparatively little-trod circuit over the

minor summit of Ptarmigan is much
more inspiring.

Follow the West Highland Way past
Rowardennan Youth Hostel to reach some
rangers' cottages. Just beyond these, an
unsigned path branches off right beside a
burn, climbing through woods and then
up a more open hillside. Below the
prominent waterfall stay left instead of
crossing a stile, following a long rising
traverse far above Loch Lomond. The path
is clear throughout, passing below small
outcrops before zigzagging steeply onto
the little grassy summit of Ptarmigan.
Follow the high ground between rocks,
pools and boggy bits, looping around the
head of a shallow corrie to reach the final
summit slopes of Ben Lomond. The path
up the steep northwest spur is rough, and

quite a slog. From the summit trig point descend via the busy normal route: this runs just below the edge of Ben Lomond's northern cliffs, and for that mountain ambience it's worth following the crest rather than the path at this stage. Where the cliff edge begins to curve northeast, drop back down to the path and follow it easily over open moorland, then through a forestry plantation, to reach Rowardennan car park. With the views at your back it would be a boring way to climb the hill, but in descent you can look down the island-studded sprawl of Loch Lomond to the distant tower blocks of Glasgow – a spectacular sight.

Munros

Munros are Scottish mountains over 3000 feet high, appearing on a list first compiled by enthusiastic climber Sir Hugh Munro in 1891. His 'Tables' have since been revised several times by the Scottish Mountaineering Club to promote or demote summits from the rankings. Currently, there are officially 284 Munros, and many more 'Tops' not thought to merit full Munro status. Arguably, the very notion of Munros is arbitrary: what's wrong with 2999-foot peaks, after all? And what objective criteria distinguish Munros from mere Tops? The list also seems rather outdated, given that mountain heights tend to be measured in metres these days (914.3m isn't such a satisfying figure as 3000 feet, however). Despite such quibbles, the popularity of Munro bagging is increasing year on year. And though they may be neglecting Scotland's many fantastic sub-3000-foot peaks, anyone who climbs all 284 Munros will certainly experience the diversity and challenge of Highland hillwalking at its best.

◀ Island-studded Loch Lomond from the lower slopes of Ben Lomond

Beinn Chabhair and An Caisteal

Beinn Chabhair (933m), **An Caisteal** (995m)
Distance 15km **Ascent** 1400m **Terrain** tracks
at first, then a long struggle on rough ground,
often pathless and with many tiring ups and
downs **Time** 6 hours 30 **Map** OS Landranger 50

If the short section of the West Highland
Way between Inverarnan and Crianlarich
seems rather too easy, try this for size.
The hills east of Inverarnan are a
confusing maze of twisting contours and
scattered outcrops. Above the grassy
knolls and peaty troughs rise fine high
summits, mountains with bags of rugged
character. This is some of the most
challenging country in the Southern
Highlands, and one of the toughest
detours described in this book. In poor
visibility the complex tangle of mini
summits west of Beinn Chabhair would
be a navigational headache even for
experienced hillwalkers, and if in doubt it
might be wise to approach the mountain
via the main path near Ben Glas Burn.

Let's assume you're on a round trip from
Inverarnan: from Beinglas Campsite
follow a small path that zigzags steeply
uphill beside the waterfall of Ben Glas
Burn to reach a broad boggy shelf at about
300m. This path leads to the summit of
Beinn Chabhair, but from the shelf it's
more fun to go off road over the obvious
bumps. Head northeast up rough, steep,
pathless ground, passing little outcrops of
banded mica schist that are worth a play if
you're into bouldering. The first mini
summit is marked by a cairn; the direct
descent is blocked by a steep wall, best
skirted to the left. Boggy hummocks now
lead over Meall Mor nan Eag to the
gorgeous hidden Lochan a' Chaisteil
nestling among crags. Unless you're drawn
by the prospect of scrambling, the next
rocky summit is easiest skirted to the
right. More energy-sapping ups and
downs lead to Stob Creag an Fhithich, a
commanding little peak. Again the direct
descent is barred by cliffs, which are best

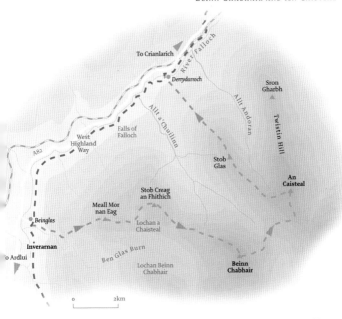

To Crianlarich

River Falloch

Derrydarroch

Sron
Gharbh

Allt Andoran

Twistin Hill

Falls of
Falloch

West
Highland
Way

A82

Allt a'Chuilinn

Stob
Glas

An
Caisteal

Stob Creag
an Fhithich

Meall Mor
nan Eag

Lochan a
Chaisteal

Beinglas

Inverarnan

Ben Glas Burn

Lochan Beinn
Chabhair

Beinn
Chabhair

o Ardlui

0   2km

avoided by looping left. Pass between crag
bands to reach the continuation over the
multiple tops of Meall nan Tarmachan
(again, watch out for crags on the descent
from each mini summit). In a tight rocky
cutting you suddenly hit the popular path,
which will come as a relief. This climbs the
bumpy northwest ridge to reach Beinn
Chabhair's summit cairn.

Descend briefly along the south ridge,
then cut northeast following a grassy
tongue that takes you down between
outcrops to reach a major low saddle: it's
easy to cut things short by walking down-
valley from here. Another rough, steep,

outcrop-weaving and practically pathless
ascent leads to the crest of An Caisteal's
south ridge – this is the most strenuous
single climb of the day. From here a good
path leads to the mountain's airy summit,
marked by a cairn. Now follow a path
down the well-defined northwest ridge,
which starts steep and rocky and
gradually becomes grassier. Hop over the
little bump of Stob Glas, then drop
northwest down pathless grassy slopes to
eventually reach the West Highland Way
at Derrydaroch. Follow this southwest
past the Falls of Falloch back to the
starting point.

◄ Lochan a' Chaisteil

Ben Lui from Dalrigh

Ben Lui (1130m) **Distance** 18km
Ascent 950m **Terrain** a foot-blisteringly long
approach on a stony track and steep mountain
path leads to a circuit of narrow exposed
ridges with some basic scrambling on
vegetated ground **Time** 8 hours
Map OS Landranger 50

With twin summits hanging gracefully
above a long, desolate glen, Ben Lui is
the monarch of the Southern Highlands.
On a day of sun and snow it looks like
it belongs in the Alps. The horseshoe
circuit of Lui's high east-facing Coire
Gaothach is a scrambly ridge walk with
a hint of mountaineering, and should be
considered a full-on winter climbing route
under snow. Less experienced hillwalkers
should save it for summer – and expect
a long day out.

Just past Dalrigh, the West Highland
Way follows a vehicle track across a
wooden bridge before turning hard right
towards Tyndrum. At this point stay with

the track, which soon passes under a
railway bridge and then goes alongside
a forestry plantation into Cononish Glen.
The track follows the north bank of the
shallow River Cononish to lonely
Cononish Farm. It now quits the river,
climbing slightly with a mine and Eas
Anie waterfall prominent on the right.
Some 2km later, the track drops back
down to the river. Ford this to reach an
old stone-walled enclosure.

A slippery path now makes a brutally
direct ascent towards Coire Gaothach,
following the course of the stream that
drains it. Pass between the corrie's
enclosing ridges to reach a group of large
boulders, which provide good shelter for
a break. Now turn left, climbing over
vegetation and little outcrops onto Ben
Lui's east ridge. Follow this, keeping just
left of the corrie rim. Initially broad and
grassy, the ground soon rises to a ragged
little false summit. Stay on easy slopes
just left of the rocks. Above is a short

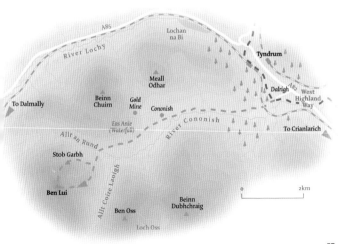

‹ Ben Lui (right) and Ben Oss from Beinn Odhar

band of broken crag, bounded on the right by the cliffs of Coire Gaothach. In summer this is a scrambly mixture of vegetation and scree. It is unavoidable, though the difficulties are pretty brief: follow an obvious line of weakness a little left of the cliff edge. The continuation to the higher of Ben Lui's twin summits is much easier. From the main top, walk the narrow crest to peak number two. Even after most of the winter snows have melted this short stretch can carry a large overhanging cornice, which you'd be crazy to go near.

The second leg of the horseshoe descends directly from peak two down the north rim of Coire Gaothach. At first steep and craggy, it soon eases off. In poor visibility or snow the initial descent might seem inadvisable. If so, a sensible alternative is to head down Ben Lui's short northwest ridge instead. This forms the back of a shallow corrie; after losing about 200m of height, leave the ridge to drop into the corrie floor near a tiny lochan. Head due east to regain the bounding ridge of Coire Gaothach at a slight saddle well below the difficult ground. From here, descend scree directly into Coire Gaothach to regain the approach path. It now takes two or three hours to walk back out to Dalrigh.

Beinn Odhar from Tyndrum

Beinn Odhar (901m) **Distance** 7km
Ascent 675m **Terrain** virtually pathless, but
unproblematic grass slopes **Time** 3 hours
Map OS Landranger 50

From below it doesn't look much, but this
grassy hump has several plus points, not
least a quick and simple ascent, and an
inspiring outlook over Tyndrum nestling
in its wooded glen, and out to the crinkly
skyline of the Crianlarich peaks. Few
Scottish hills this size are so easily won.

Follow the West Highland Way north
out of Tyndrum for about 1.5km.
Immediately after it crosses the railway

on a little old bridge, leave the track and
head NNE. There is barely a trace of a
path, but then one isn't really needed
since the way is obvious – simply go up.
Climb bumpy grassy slopes – boggy in
parts – to eventually reach the scattered
spoil of some old mine workings on the
crest of the mountain's southern spur.
The dank little mine openings are worth
a quick look for those with troglodytic
tendencies. Continue up the spur, mostly
grassy underfoot, crossing a dilapidated
fence and passing a pool. The final
summit cone demands a steep pull up
stony slopes, though the hard work is

short lived. For a relatively minor peak that doesn't seem to see much traffic, the summit cairn is surprisingly substantial. To the north is Beinn Dorain, dwarfing the railway and the West Highland Way. Return the way you came.

Glaciation

The Ice Age began about 2.5 million years ago. Since then temperatures have risen and fallen periodically, creating waves of glaciation and non-glaciated warm phases – we are in one of these at the present time. Sometimes the Scottish mountains hosted only small glaciers in high valleys, while in other phases ice sheets several kilometres thick covered most of northern Europe. Scotland's last glaciers melted around 11,500 years ago, but their effects are still clearly visible. Glaciers played a major role in sculpting the mountain landforms we see today, gouging out deep corries, chiselling ridgelines, ploughing along lower glens to create typical post-glacial 'U-shaped' valleys and digging deep troughs that have since become lochs. The eroded material was deposited as moraines, gravel mounds that underlie the grassy hummocks to be found in many lower glens today. Big boulders standing alone in seemingly random places are glacial 'erratics', once carried along by moving ice.

Beinn Odhar and the Crianlarich peaks from Beinn Dorain

59

Beinn Dorain from Bridge of Orchy

Beinn Dorain (1076m) **Distance** 12km
Ascent 930m **Terrain** a well-used path to the
top, then the option of a steep, rough descent
that requires care **Time** 5 hours
Map OS Landranger 50

**One of the West Highland Way's really
iconic landmarks**, Beinn Dorain combines
a fairly straightforward climb with the
option of a more arduous descent (as
described here). Tracing the distinctive
profiles of the Crianlarich peaks, Ben Lui,
Ben Cruachan and the Black Mount, the
summit panorama is magnificent. Dorain
is most commonly climbed as a round
trip from Bridge of Orchy. With a short
detour the neighbouring Munro Beinn an
Dothaidh can also be visited.

Follow the southbound West Highland
Way out of Bridge of Orchy. Just beyond
the station underpass take a path on the
left, past a telecom transmitter. Climb

steadily eastwards through grassy
hummocks, beside the cutting of the Allt
Coire an Dothaidh. The path – quite
boggy in places – ascends into the bowl of
Coire an Dothaidh, climbing steeply and
stonily between two large crags to reach a
saddle at 744m, marked by a cairn. This is
the jumping-off point for a detour to
Beinn an Dothaidh.

For Dorain, turn hard right on a stony
path up a spur. Pass a pool on a flatter
area before climbing more steeply again,
weaving up onto the broad north ridge.
The first summit you reach is graced with
two big cairns, and thus easily mistaken
for the true summit. The highest point is
actually a little further south across a
notch. Ringed by breakneck craggy slopes,
it feels like a genuine mountain top.

To descend, the less sure-footed would
be advised to retrace their steps to Bridge
of Orchy. Sturdy adventurous types might

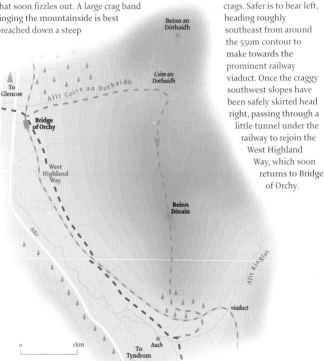

◄ West Highland railway from the southern slopes of Beinn Dorain

prefer the off-road option. The descent due south is a worthwhile undertaking, and though it is pretty rough underfoot it does have the benefit of directness. It would be murder in ascent. Weave down through bands of rock on a path that soon fizzles out. A large crag band ringing the mountainside is best breached down a steep grassy gully, requiring some care. Below the crags is a boulder field. Once you've teetered down this, you reach steep grass slopes. A direct descent to the West Highland Way isn't recommended as it runs into many little broken crags. Safer is to bear left, heading roughly southeast from around the 550m contour to make towards the prominent railway viaduct. Once the craggy southwest slopes have been safely skirted head right, passing through a little tunnel under the railway to rejoin the West Highland Way, which soon returns to Bridge of Orchy.

To Glencoe

Allt Coire an Dothaidh

Bridge of Orchy

West Highland Way

A82

Beinn an Dòthaidh

Coire an Dothaidh

Beinn Dòrain

Allt Kinglas

viaduct

0   1km

Auch

To Tyndrum

Glen Orchy and Beinn Udlaidh

Beinn Udlaidh (840m), **Beinn Bhreac-liath** (802m) **Distance** 17km **Ascent** 930m **Terrain** some tarmac, some track and a lot of near pathless grassy hillside **Time** 5 hours 30 **Map** OS Landranger 50

From the West Highland Way the rounded lump of Beinn Udlaidh (pron. Ood-ly) is almost invisible, and hardly looks worth the effort. Small it may be, but this mountain rises in proud isolation. Ringed at a distance by some of the highest peaks in the Southern Highlands, it is a great viewpoint. Moistened by a series of springs on the summit plateau, Udlaidh's northern cliffs are a regular ice factory in winter, requiring only a brief freeze to produce fabulous ice routes, a magnet for climbers. However, few hillwalkers seem to bother with Beinn Udlaidh and the neighbouring Corbett Beinn Bhreac-liath, so for most of

the year they are rarely busy.

From the A82 just south of Bridge of Orchy, turn left onto the B8074 for a long stretch on tarmac, following the beautiful river in the base of Glen Orchy as far as Glen Orchy Farm. Here cross a muddy field to take the rough 4WD track into forestry plantations, climbing steeply through the trees roughly parallel to the Allt Daim to emerge in the lower reaches of Coire Daimh. Tiers of cliffs on the corrie's back wall form a strikingly symmetrical semicircle, and if it's winter they may well be festooned in ice. The track climbs the broad west arm enclosing the corrie, steering well clear of the crags. The steep spur soon rolls back onto a gentle summit plateau scattered with stones, bogs and tiny pools. It's this general dampness that makes Beinn Udlaidh such a superb winter ice-climbing

venue. The track peters into a path, which curves to the northeast to reach the mountain's highest point. Here there's an impressive cairn, and a rather less attractive communications mast mounted on a rusty Heath-Robinson trailer.

On a clear day the view takes in the perfect cone of Beinn Dorain, the Black Mount and Ben Cruachan's clutch of pointy tops. Continue southeast from the cairn, rounding the craggy rim of Coire

Ghamhnain to descend to the col at its head. A steep climb brings you to the summit of Beinn Bhreac-liath. Follow its broad north ridge to make a long descent back to the minor road about 1km from the A82 junction.

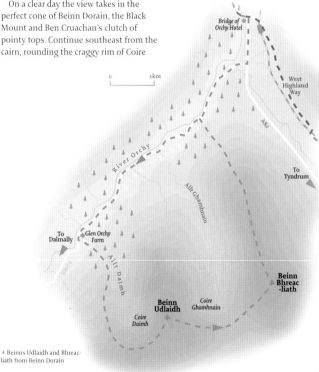

Bridge of Orchy Hotel

West Highland Way

A82

To Tyndrum

River Orchy

Allt Ghamhnain

To Dalmally

Glen Orchy Farm

Allt Daimh

Beinn Udlaidh

Coire Ghamhnain

Beinn Bhreac -liath

Coire Daimh

0   1km

◄ Beinns Udlaidh and Bhreac-liath from Beinn Dorain

Stob Ghabhar and the Black Mount

Stob Ghabhar (1090m) **Distance** 16km
Ascent 970m **Terrain** rough ground, exposed
ridges and some optional hard scrambling
Time 7 hours **Map** OS Landranger 50

Rising over the wild flatlands of Rannoch
Moor, Stob Ghabhar is magnificent. It is
best approached from Forest Lodge on the
West Highland Way. The first treat is the
impressive waterfall at the lip of Coire na
Mhuic – though visible for miles, only up
close is its scale apparent. The buttress
above offers an optional grade 3 scramble –
good fun, but easily avoided. The
continuation ridge Aonach Eagach (not to
be confused with its more famous Glencoe
namesake) narrows unexpectedly to form
an airy arête, rimming a rugged, secluded

corrie that holds snow late into spring.
This is Scottish hillwalking at its finest.

From Forest Lodge, take a track beside
the Abhainn Shira. A small hut marks the
turn-off path alongside the Allt Toaig,
which you follow for about 1.5km. Leave
the main path at the burn draining Coire
na Mhuic, climbing just right of the rocky
cascades (these provide a scramble, if
you're so inclined). Above these, head
north across the boggy corrie floor.
There is now a choice. If you want to
scramble, aim for the craggy terminal
nose of Aonach Eagach which is climbed
on slabby rock staying slightly right of
the steep stuff. Alternatively, skirt left of
the rock to climb rough slopes leading
to the crest of Aonach Eagach. Turn left

◀ Stob Ghabhar and Loch Tulla at dawn

to ascend the ridge, with one fairly exposed section just before the summit of Stob Ghabhar.

Descend northwest around the head of the corrie to reach the grassy ridge of Sron nan Giubhas. This is abruptly cut short at an awkward descent on mossy rock – caution when wet. With care it is then possible to descend to the corrie floor at a boggy levelling just downstream of the

lochan, from where a rough climb over the small pass west of Stob a' Choire Odhair regains the approach path. However, it is also feasible to continue down off the very end of Sron nan Giubhas (avoiding any outcrops), from where a northward leg across the moor brings you to a rough path along the north bank of the River Ba (cross carefully if it's in spate): this leads to the West Highland Way at Ba Bridge.

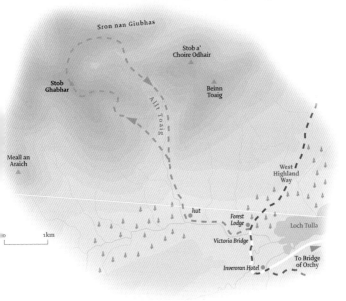

A Rannoch Moor viewpoint

Beinn Chaorach (475m) **Distance** 2km
Ascent 75m **Terrain** pathless moorland, rough
and very soggy **Time** 45 minutes
Map OS Landranger 41

If the walk between Bridge of Orchy
and Kingshouse is feeling more like a
busy caravan of walkers than the isolated
experience you had hoped for, then you
may appreciate a quick dip into a world of
silence, with only deer for company.
The short diversion from the West
Highland Way to the minor summit of
Beinn Chaorach gives a sense of the scale
of Rannoch Moor, and gets up close and
personal with its inhospitable terrain.
A pair of gaiters would be welcome.

Coming from the south, quit the West
Highland Way at a bridge just short of the
high point between Ba Bridge and the ski

'A wearier-looking desert man never saw'

A plateau at 300m altitude and more than 16km across, ringed by high hills and pitted with peat bogs, lochans and streams, Rannoch Moor is one of the most forbidding and evocative landscapes in Scotland. An ice sheet once covered the whole area, draining down glaciers in side valleys such as Glencoe and Glen Etive; there's still a distinctive Arctic tundra-like feel to the place. The moor may seem a sterile environment, but its extensive blanket bogs are actually a rare habitat for threatened plants and animals. The waterlogged terrain proves hard going for any would-be traveller; when the builders of the West Highland Line came to push the railway through in the late 19th century, long stretches of track had to be floated on a mat of tree roots and earth. Corrour Station at the northern tip of the moor famously featured in the cult film *Trainspotting*. Other cultural associations include a bit part in Robert Louis Stevenson's *Kidnapped*, in which the hero complains that 'a wearier-looking desert man never saw'. In fierce weather it can seem like the end of the Earth, but catch it in a good mood and Rannoch Moor is stunning.

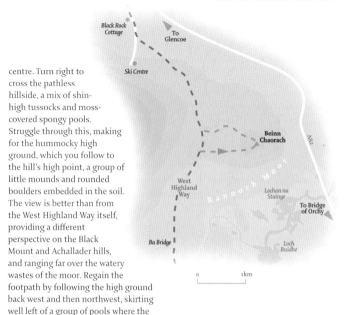

centre. Turn right to cross the pathless hillside, a mix of shin-high tussocks and moss-covered spongy pools. Struggle through this, making for the hummocky high ground, which you follow to the hill's high point, a group of little mounds and rounded boulders embedded in the soil. The view is better than from the West Highland Way itself, providing a different perspective on the Black Mount and Achallader hills, and ranging far over the watery wastes of the moor. Regain the footpath by following the high ground back west and then northwest, skirting well left of a group of pools where the going is particularly soggy.

˅ Rannoch Moor

Buachaille Etive Mor

Buachaille Etive Mor (Stob Dearg) (1022m)
Distance 5km **Ascent** 740m **Terrain** mostly
a good path, but some steep, loose ground
in both ascent and descent **Time** 3 hours
Map OS Landranger 41 or Harvey British
Mountain Map (1:40,000) Ben Nevis
& Glen Coe

Standing proud between the mouth of
Glencoe and the flats of Rannoch Moor,
the great rock pyramid of Buachaille Etive
Mor has one of the most recognisable
mountain profiles in Scotland. Star of a
thousand postcards, the Big Herdsman of
Etive is the single most impressive object
on the West Highland Way. It is a sight to
make a keen climber's palms tingle with
vicarious excitement. 'The Buachaille', as
it is called by devotees, may look

impregnable to the likes of lowly walkers,
but if scrabbling around on exposed
rockfaces is not your bag there is another
way up. The bowl of Coire na Tulaich
breaches the mountain's formidable
defences to provide a short but sharp
there-and-back route.

From Altnafeadh farm beside the A82
and the West Highland Way, take the track
south to a footbridge over the River
Coupall. On the far bank is a path past the
white climbing club cottage of
Lagangarbh. Where the path forks keep
right, climbing gently at first and passing
some rock slabs on the left to enter Coire
na Tulaich. The path follows the burn
cutting until the corrie floor soon
becomes a steep scree slope. The climb
used to be purgatory until a path upgrade
improved matters; eventually, however,
the stone steps of the path peter out,
leaving you with a last steep grind up a

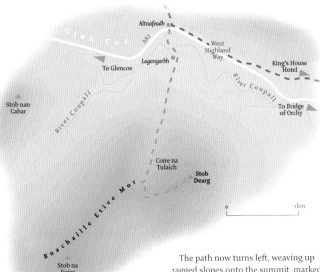

The path now turns left, weaving up ragged slopes onto the summit, marked by a cairn. From here the true scale of Rannoch Moor is dramatically apparent, with the miniature A82 cutting a straight course over it into the hazy distance. Return the way you came, taking great care to locate the correct descent into Coire na Tulaich if it's misty.

precarious loose bit onto the saddle above the head of the corrie. In winter the exit slopes may carry snow cornices, and can also be dangerously avalanche prone – in these conditions, give it a miss.

Scottish climbing

For Scottish climbers, Buachaille Etive Mor is hallowed ground. From the late 19th century – when, incidentally, access to the King's House at its foot was still by horse-drawn cart along a rough track – the mountain was occupied a prominent place in the climbing exploits of every generation. First to pioneer routes here were doughty Victorian gents such as Naismith and Collie, with ascents of obvious features such as Great Gully, North Buttress and Crowberry Ridge. New routes have been forced on The Buachaille's cliffs and gullies ever since, both on summer rock and winter snow and ice. Established classics of every level of difficulty continue to be a magnet to climbers – on a fine day, look hard and you might spot ant-like figures high on the crags.

Blackwater Dam from Kinlochleven

Distance 13km **Ascent** 350m **Terrain** a good path on the way to the dam, but some potentially tricky burn crossings in the rain. The return leg follows a unique concrete culvert **Time** 4 hours 30 **Map** OS Landranger 41 or Harvey British Mountain Map (1:40,000) Ben Nevis & Glen Coe

A stroll up the glen from Kinlochleven to the Blackwater Dam takes in a variety of contrasting scenes – pretty birch woodland, open moorland, rushing waterfalls and industrial heritage on a vast scale. In a rainy spell, the glen comes alive with the roar of white water. Wet or dry, this is one of the most underrated low-level walks in the Highlands.

From the north side of the bridge over the River Leven in Kinlochleven, take the riverside path east through trees. Beyond a housing estate is a footpath through birches, signed for the Blackwater Reservoir. After about 1km, you pass a multiple waterfall just above the path. In the woods below, the main river foams through its rocky gorge. Descend to a footbridge over a side stream. With a large waterfall to your left, climb through the trees, which begin to thin as you pass an old ruin, fording several minor burns to reach the Allt Coire na Duibhe. As it drains a large boggy catchment area this can prove exciting in full flood, and is always worth treating with respect as you hop across the burn. Occasionally it is impassable: take no chances. Beyond the stream, a further 2km of uphill effort brings you to the dam and reservoir,

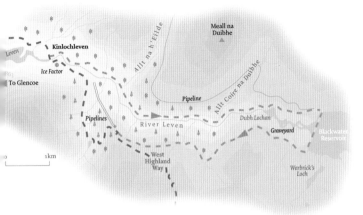

a huge ribbon of water in a barren expanse of nothingness. At nearly 1km long and just under 30m high the dam was once the biggest in Europe, and though it no longer feeds the aluminium works for which the project was originally built it does still provide electricity for local residents a full century after it went into service. How many contemporary engineering marvels will stand the test of time so well?

Though it looks like it would make an ideal pathway the dam is officially off limits, so if that sort of thing bothers you then cross the river shallows below it and make for an old boarded-up house at its opposite end. The nearby graveyard for dam workers is a moving sight. On a day of moody weather this is an atmospheric

spot – spooky, even. You could almost fancy that the wind rippling these cold waters is the sigh of the ghosts of the navvies who perished here: OK, maybe that's stretching things a bit. Now feeling a little edgy and checking over your shoulder every few seconds, find the concrete conduit that carries water from the reservoir. Snaking along the glen's steep southern slopes, sometimes with a sheer drop-off one side or another, it's a novel and entertaining way to return, and you'll wish you'd carried a bike up just to enjoy this bit. Eventually the conduit reaches the house at the top of the aluminium works pipelines, where you rejoin the West Highland Way for the long, looping track back into town.

◀ Blackwater Reservoir in the wastes of Rannoch Moor

Into the Mamores

Binnein Mor (1130m), **Na Gruagaichean** (1055m) **Distance** 15km **Ascent** 1350m **Terrain** some good paths, narrow stony ridges and rough descents **Time** 7 hours **Map** OS Landranger 41 or Harvey British Mountain Map (1:40,000) Ben Nevis & Glen Coe

The high soaring ridges and chiselled peaks of the Mamores give graceful walks, routes with an airy feel and typically stirring Lochaber backdrops. This full-bore hill day visits the highest point in the range, a remote summit reached via fairly rough ground. It's an ideal first taste of Mamores ridge bashing. There's plenty more where that came from – the celebrated Ring of Steall, for instance (accessed from Glen Nevis). With a bit of tinkering the route can be modified into a high-level approach to Glen Nevis, an exciting – if strenuous – alternative to Stage 8 of the West Highland Way.

From the car park beside a small church in Kinlochmore (the north half of Kinlochleven), head northeast out of town on a woodland path. Where this splits stay right (the left branch heads to the Grey Mare's Tail waterfall, of which more later) to climb onto an open grassy shoulder with good views along the length of Loch Leven. The path eventually meets a contouring 4WD track. It resumes beyond this track, a little way to the left. The path now climbs over a boggy slope to enter desolate Coire nan Laogh. Cross two burns, then make a steep rising traverse across the south flank of Sgurr Eilde Beag. As the path levels out, look for a left branch marked by a cairn. The well-engineered zigzags of this old stalker's path make light work of the uncompromising Sgurr Eilde Beag.

From the stony summit follow the northern cliff edge over a minor col, picking up signs of passing boots that lead up a grassy slope to the unnamed 1062m

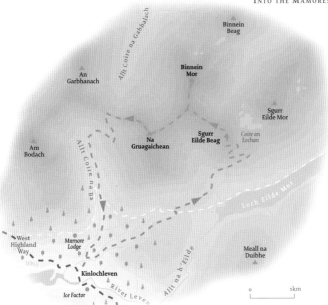

top, marked with a cairn. Binnein Mor deserves the 30-minute round trip. Follow the narrow ridge northwards over grass and quartzite blocks to reach its commanding summit, then return from whence you came. Back at the 1062m top, descend southwest on stony ground. The ridge narrows over a col, becoming quite ragged as it leads up on to Na Gruagaichean: a path stays just left of the crest to avoid all scrambling. From the airy peak, carefully drop northwest into a tight little notch before climbing quite abruptly to the second grassier summit. A long descent on a well-scuffed path leads to the lowest bealach in the Mamores range.

A cairn marks the Kinlochleven-bound path. This path meanders but eventually straightens out and reaches the lower glen; shortcutting the woods would be unpleasantly steep. About 3km from the bealach, meet the 4WD track again. Turn left onto this for a very short distance, being careful not to miss a path on the right, often masked by bracken. This descends through open heathland. Bear left at a junction, dropping steeply into the woods to meet the Grey Mare's Tail path. The waterfall is only a two-minute detour, and worth a look on the way back to Kinlochleven.

◀ Looking over the Mamores

Nevis Gorge and Steall Falls

Distance 9km **Ascent** 170m **Terrain** easy
paths and some tarmac **Time** 3 hours
Map OS Landranger 41 or Harvey British
Mountain Map (1:40,000) Ben Nevis
& Glen Coe

Glen Nevis is one of the grandest valleys
in Scotland, befitting its position at the
foot of our highest mountain. Woods,
crags, waterfalls and a towering skyline
comprising the Mamores, Ben Nevis and
the mighty Aonachs – it has it all. If the
peaks are shrouded in cloud or your legs
threaten to go on strike at the prospect
of yet another hill, head up-glen for some
of the finest and most accessible scenery
in the area.

Travel by foot, thumb or bus (summer
service) up the minor road past the youth
hostel to the falls at Polldubh. These are
impressive in spate. Where the road
makes a sharp bend over a bridge above
the falls, go right through a gate to follow
a well-made gravel trail on the south side
of the Water of Nevis. This stays close to
the pretty riverbank with the scattered
crags of the Glen Nevis climbing area
prominent across the glen. Beyond some
small rapids, the path climbs slightly
through birches to reach a footbridge.
Cross to the north side of the river here,
as the continuation along the south bank
is best avoided: it starts very boggy
before petering into frustratingly difficult
ground. Follow the quiet dead-end road
to the car park at its end, close to a big
waterslide that pours off the flanks
of Ben Nevis.

◀ Glen Nevis Gorge

A sign marks the onward path up the glen, and though it warns of doom and gloom it is in reality a gentle stroll, and you'd have to be trying extremely hard – and probably drunk – to take a fatal fall. As you climb through native woods the glen makes an abrupt right turn, narrowing into a tight gorge choked with huge boulders through which the river roars: it's a distinctly impressive spot. Above the gorge, the valley opens onto an unexpected floodplain ringed by woods and steep mountainsides down which pour the 100m Steall Falls, one of Scotland's biggest. To see the cascade at close quarters, you have to re-cross the Water of Nevis via an excitingly wobbly wire bridge – one cable to walk on, and one for each hand. If you pass this test without getting soaked, then the bogs on the far side will finish you off. Return the way you came.

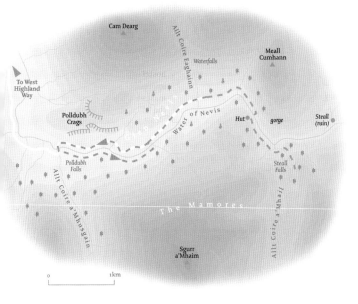

Ben Nevis via the Tourist Track

Ben Nevis (1344m) **Distance** 12km (starting at visitor centre) **Ascent** 1334m
Terrain a straightforward but very long path, a lot of it pretty rough underfoot. On the summit plateau you may experience anything from T-shirt weather and 100km views to pea soup visibility, gales, snow and a navigational headache. Expect the worst **Time** 5 hours
Map OS Landranger 41 or Harvey British Mountain Map (1:40,000) Ben Nevis & Glen Coe

Ben Nevis is a mountain for everyone – people of all ages, backgrounds and nationalities. Rising out of leafy Glen Nevis to the distant stony summit, the Tourist Track must be Scotland's most trodden path. This is the only 'easy' route, and you're as likely to see people dressed for the High Street as for the hills. Stilettos might not be ideally suited to the terrain, yet their use isn't unknown. After a day on the Ben, nothing will surprise you.

Start either from Glen Nevis Youth Hostel or from the visitor centre car park closer to Fort William. The former is steeper, the latter slightly further. Both routes meet up at about the 160m contour. The flagstone-surfaced path then makes a long rising traverse above Glen Nevis, crossing a couple of little bridges before curving left into a side valley. It climbs steeply to reach a long easy incline near the 'Halfway Lochan' (Lochan Meall an t-Suidhe). You might be disappointed to learn that the name isn't strictly accurate.

So far the path surface has been impeccable, but where the track does an abrupt hairpin by a short length of wall it becomes much more rough and stony, and continues thus all the way to the top. The hard work has only just begun: it's even worse in descent! There follows a seemingly endless series of zigzags. Thankfully the views over lochs and mountains really begin to open out as a reward for the hard graft. Pass into a moonscape of rubble, edging closer to the lip of the north face as you follow a string

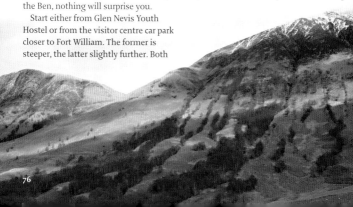

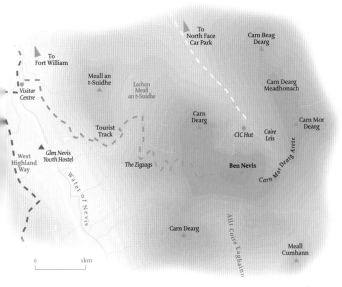

To
North Face
Car Park

Carn Beag
Dearg

To
Fort William

Meall an
t-Suidhe

Lochan
Meall
an t-Suidhe

Carn Dearg
Meadhonach

Visitor
Centre

Carn
Dearg

Carn Mor
Dearg

Tourist
Track

CIC Hut

Coire
Leis

West
Highland
Way

Glen Nevis
Youth Hostel

Ben Nevis

The Zigzags

Carn Mor Dearg Arete

Water of Nevis

Carn Dearg

Allt Coire Eoghainn

Meall
Cumhann

0   1km

of cairns across the barren plateau. Reach the cliff edge near the head of a steep gully, steering well clear of any snow cornices that could collapse unexpectedly. Beyond a second gully the path makes a sharp left turn to reach the ruined observatory, trig point and emergency shelter.

Descend the way you came. The plateau is ringed on almost every side by steep ground, and deeply incised by dangerous gullies. On a sunny day you might wonder what the fuss is about, but in mist it is vital to strike the correct line, especially if the path is invisible under snow. From the summit trig point, follow a compass bearing of 231° grid for 150m, watching out for the head of the gully on your right;

carry on descending on a bearing of 281° grid for a further 1km or so, to be sure that you're safely on the zigzags. It's worth being religious about this, because unseen on your left is the head of Five Finger Gully, an accident blackspot that it's disconcertingly easy to stray into. Shortcuts straighten out some of the bends of the meandering main path, but take the wrong one and you'll end up descending quite far right, beside the Red Burn. In summer this is unpleasant scree; in winter it's sometimes an avalanche hazard. Compared with Five Finger Gully on the one hand and the Red Burn on the other, the Tourist Track's knee-numbing zigzags are the lesser of three evils.

◄ The southern slopes of Ben Nevis

Ben Nevis via CMD Arête

Ben Nevis (1344m) **Distance** 15km
Ascent 1650m **Terrain** rough paths, a steep
pathless ascent and a narrow rocky ridge with
some very easy scrambling **Time** 8 hours
Map OS Landranger 41 or Harvey British
Mountain Map (1:40,000) Ben Nevis
& Glen Coe

For ambitious mountain walkers, this is
the route to the top of Ben Nevis. A world
away from the crowded (and frankly
rather dull) Tourist Track, the Carn Mor
Dearg Arête is an exciting and physically
demanding walk, and the grandest
mountain day described in this book. The
crest connecting Carn Mor Dearg and Ben
Nevis is a dramatic aerial walkway with an
unequalled perspective on the huge crags
of the Ben's wild side. The actual hands-
on scrambling may be limited, but the
position is superb.

Follow the Tourist Track to the Halfway
Lochan. At the tight hairpin mentioned

in the previous route, turn off left on a
horizontal path, recently engineered to
give the easiest walking of the day.
Continue until a mucky old path branches
right, following this over boggy moorland
below the scree slopes of Carn Dearg to
enter the Allt a'Mhuilinn valley. The path
descends slightly below the first rock wall
of the Ben's sprawling north face, then
climbs gradually towards the CIC Hut
(not a public bothy). Just short of the
hut cross the burn, and the main Allt
a'Mhuilinn path, and head straight up
the slopes of Carn Dearg Meadhonach,
uncompromisingly steep grass and
scree all the way. If you manage to find
something masquerading as a path
you'll soon lose it again. The summit
of Carn Dearg Meadhonach comes as a
relief – eventually.

With an ever-changing view of the
Ben's complex tangle of buttresses and
gullies, follow the stony crest onto Carn

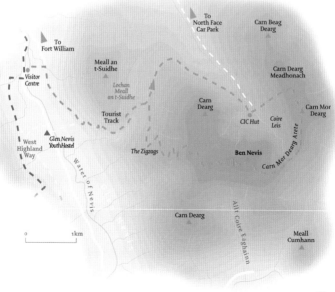

‹ CMD Arête and the North East Buttress of Ben Nevis, from Carn Mor Dearg

Mor Dearg. Beyond this pointy summit the fun begins, a narrow arête of rounded blocks sweeping around the head of the corrie in a great arc. A path weaves below the rock steps, but sticking to the crest is more pleasant and gives the occasional scrambly moment. After a tight right kink the ridge drops to a low point of 1058m before climbing to meet the main mass of Ben Nevis at a point marked by an abseil post (not a recommended descent).

A calf-bursting slog up a rubble slope follows, the best route staying sensibly left of the lip of the Brenva Face, as marked by an intermittent line of metal posts. This brings you, after rather too long, to the summit plateau. Descend via the Tourist Track, being careful to follow the advice in the previous route in poor visibility, and counting your blessings you didn't come up this way.

Directory